Praise for **create togetherness.**

"In *Create Togetherness*, Jeff Davis goes beyond just facts and figures to help business leaders deeply understand why and where the sales and marketing relationship breaks down. Jeff brings a fresh and unique perspective that helps B2B marketing and sales leaders understand how they can finally and sustainably align. This book is immensely valuable for any c-suite executive looking to position their organization for growth."

— Mary Shea,
Ph.D., Principal Analyst, Forrester Research

"Sellers and marketers must be aligned and in agreement on their buyers' needs in order to meet revenue goals. Jeff Davis understands deeply what it means for sales and marketing teams to achieve this, and *Create Togetherness* is a great representation of that. Whether at a company that is struggling with misalignment, or one that simply wants to help take their go-to-market teams to the next level, readers will find a lot of value in this book."

— Ed Calnan,
President and Founder, Seismic

"I'm so excited that Jeff Davis wrote *Create Togetherness*. He continues to be at the forefront of helping B2B leaders transform their thinking about sales and marketing. It is not easy to do so, but he pulls it off by having the tough conversations and speaking plainly about the changes that have to happen to win a modern buyer."

— Trish Bertuzzi,
CEO, The Bridge Group, Inc.,
author of *The Sales Development Playbook*

"*Create Togetherness* is a must-read for any company leader who wants to win in today's complex B2B selling environment. Jeff Davis offers an extremely unique perspective on alignment that will resonate with both sales and marketing leaders because of his extensive experience in both fields. Alignment is the future of B2B, and Jeff does a stellar job of showing us how to get there."

— Roderick Jefferson,
CEO, Roderick Jefferson & Associates, LLC

"Jeff Davis has an amazing way of helping sales and marketing leaders understand how they can become better partners in order to close more deals, faster. He is without a doubt an authority when it comes to helping B2B organizations transform their sales and marketing teams into a high-performing Revenue Engine and *Create Togetherness* proves that fact."

— Brian Everett,
CEO, Transportation Marketing and Sales Association

"The ageless battle between sales and marketing has led both functions to underperform and under-contribute for too long. Finally, Jeff Davis offers a wonderful solution for leaders and members of both functions to come together and create competitive capabilities neither function could on their own. His blueprint for co-creating an integrated revenue machine will enable sales and marketing leaders to thrive in areas where they've long floundered. If you are a sales or marketing leader, keep this book handy on the edge of your desk. You'll be so glad you did."

— Ron Carucci,
bestselling author of *Rising to Power: The Journey of Exceptional Executives*, and Managing Partner at Navalent

create togetherness.

Transform Sales and Marketing to Exceed Modern Buyers' Expectations and Increase Revenue

create togetherness.

Transform Sales and Marketing to Exceed Modern Buyers' Expectations and Increase Revenue

JEFF DAVIS

PUBLISHING

Create Togetherness: Transform Sales and Marketing To Exceed Buyers' Expectations and Increase Revenue

Book Editing by Lindsey Parker Novak
Book Design by Ben VanderVeen
Book Layout by Douglas Williams

ISBN 978-1-7334504-0-9   Paperback
ISBN 978-1-7334504-1-6   eBook

For ordering information or special discounts for bulk/corporate purchases, please contact JD2 Publishing, LLC at 708.628.7913 or jeff@jeffdavis2.com

www.meetjeffdavis.com | www.TheAlignmentPodcast.com

To Ella Davis-Greer for her unwavering support of people achieving their highest potential. For me, you have made all of this possible. I love you, mom.

"Sales and marketing leaders will continue to see the increasing importance of building a Revenue Engine that aligns both teams' efforts as the only way to connect with the modern buyer. The way buyers interact with B2B companies is in the midst of a seismic shift. Those leaders who commit to an alignment transformation will be winners in the new B2B economy. Those who don't will be at a stark disadvantage."

— **Jeff Davis,**
Founder & CEO,
JD2 Consulting Group

Contents

Foreword

FROM THE SALES LEADER

Every sales leader knows it's become more challenging to achieve revenue growth in today's complex B2B selling environment. With the modern buyer demanding a more cohesive and seamless buying experience, many leaders are starting to realize they must find a better way for sales and marketing to work together.

Jeff Davis intimately understands how to transform sales and marketing into better strategic alignment. He leverages his professional experience of 15+ years in sales, marketing, and business development from Fortune 100 companies to early-stage startups. His passion for improving the relationship between sales, marketing, and the modern buyer have led him to exclusively focus his energy on helping companies build high-performing Revenue Engines.

Davis is definitely the go-to resource when B2B leaders want to better understand how to align their teams. Through keynoting conferences, producing the TheAlignmentPodcast.com, and delivering hands-on executive workshops, he consistently produces highly valuable thought leadership that inspires leaders to shift their mindset and approach to the sales and marketing relationship.

His book *Create Togetherness* is a perfect example of his passion and commitment to fundamentally changing the way B2B organizations approach sales and marketing, as well as the customer experience. Davis empowers B2B leaders with actionable insights, frameworks, templates, and other business tools that create clarity for when they decide to begin the alignment transformation journey in their organizations.

As a sales leader, it's exciting to have a resource like this who provides a blueprint for how sales leaders should approach leveraging their marketing team to more effectively and consistently hit revenue targets in the modern B2B selling environment.

— Craig Wortmann,
CEO, Sales Engine Inc.,
Clinical Professor of Innovation & Entrepreneurship,
Founder & Executive Director of the Kellogg Sales Institute
Kellogg School of Management at Northwestern University,
and Operating Partner, Pritzker Group Venture Capital

FROM THE MARKETING LEADER

Sales and marketing alignment is an age-old topic that continues to be a major challenge for B2B companies. There have been many studies showing how lack of alignment is a huge blocker to revenue growth for companies — and conversely — can be a major competitive advantage when done right. In *Create Togetherness,* Jeff Davis brings keen insight to helping leaders see why this conflict continues to be dysfunctional. He then offers a clear path to improving sales and marketing collaboration and shows how to empower leaders to transform sales and marketing into one team focused on growth.

Jeff Davis taps into his unique expertise and fresh perspective to create a book that clearly lays out the business case for why alignment is worth the time, energy, and effort. He relies on his background from a variety of organizations of all sizes to shed light on what companies can do to improve. This includes breaking down the silos between sales and marketing and showing that, by focusing on the customer and their buying experience, companies can align their teams.

Davis not only evangelizes alignment, he provides real value by sharing examples, stories, business tools, and more to help leaders create meaningful change in their organizations.

It is such a pleasure to have a business leader of Jeff Davis' caliber focused on such an important and relevant topic for every B2B business leader today. This book creates a real opportunity for sales and marketing leaders, as well as CEOs, to start an authentic conversation about alignment and make change happen.

— Tracy Eiler,
CMO, InsideView
and author of *Aligned to Achieve*, Wiley 2016

Preface

"Do the difficult things while they are easy and do the great things while they are small. A journey of a thousand miles must begin with a single step."

— Lao Tzu

Why did I write a book on the need for aligning sales and marketing? I had worked in both areas and became frustrated with the two departments not understanding their value to one another. I reached a point in my career where I felt compelled to speak out and help companies resolve the disconnect before it destroyed their ability to compete in the new B2B marketplace. I had to use all means possible to help resolve this breakdown, whether it was through a book, as a speaker, on a podcast, or getting into the trenches as a consultant to help transform companies. My engineering background wouldn't allow me to stop obsessing that there had to be a better way for marketing and sales to work together, especially since I've been on both sides. I repeatedly saw missed opportunities because sales and marketing weren't working as a team within a cohesive revenue-generating system. And so my journey led me to explore how to align these two functions. When I couldn't easily see the answers, I was motivated to better understand why the system was broken and what could be done to create sustainable change.

One experience in particular changed the way I saw the relationship between sales and marketing. It was this "aha" moment that confirmed that this relationship had to experience a major transformation to end misalignment.

As a sales representative for several years after receiving my bachelor's degree in engineering, I attended our usual district sales meeting, where I had planned to talk about the same issues we always discussed – how the district was performing, how we could work together better, best practices, blah blah blah. I was prepared to contribute to the discussion and to be fully engaged. I wanted my manager to hear my opinions and know I was focused on finding a solution. At the same time, I was counting down the hours for the meeting to end and lamenting over my preferring to be in the field calling on customers. Instead, I was at a sales meeting with my colleagues, so I felt determined to put on a show.

What I didn't know was that something would happen in that meeting to forever change the way I saw the relationship between sales and marketing. Until that point, I never had contact with marketing outside of receiving their sales content directing us (the sales professionals) to talk about the product as they thought best, and to hear their strategy at our company-wide meetings on the main stage. As a salesperson, I didn't really understand what marketing did.

The meeting started as usual. We had our morning coffee and engaged in catching-up with our team. The district sales manager then reviewed our district and individual territory performances. This is where we prayed we weren't at the bottom of any list to avoid being singled out. After going through performance, our district sales manager announced we had a special guest joining us from the marketing department. All our expressions showed concern. What did we do wrong?

The special guest was introduced, and again our expressions said, "Uh oh, someone from corporate is here. Look like you know what you are talking about." But his presentation proved to be vastly different from what we expected.

The marketing leader (Mark – not his real name) immediately established credibility. "I'm here to share with you how we, as the marketing team, are here to partner with you and support you in building better relationships with your customers."

I questioned what I was hearing since no one from marketing had ever shared or treated sales as a partner.

He continued: "We know it's been challenging to drive sales in the current environment, and we want to help you by helping shape the market and develop tools that educate your customers on why they should be choosing your products."

I had to express my surprise and gratitude. "Really excited to have you join us today."

Marketing had been the Ivory Tower that disseminated our orders. The idea of partnering with marketing was foreign, but I was all ears to hear what he had to say. He explained how they had created a new tool to help us identify the different types of customers, how best to sell to them, what they cared about, the best messaging to use, how to emotionally connect with them, the best resources to share with them to offer proof, and that using this tool would help us be more efficient in targeting the right buyers.

Whoa! This was a game-changer for me. I instantly saw how this tool would improve my performance and I planned on using it the next day.

Now, as a marketer, I understand what Mark and his team had done. He wanted to share with the sales team the customer persona research that was generated by marketing. They translated the work into a relevant context for salespeople to improve targeting and interactions with customers, which would ultimately lead to increased sales.

The alignment solution hit me. I finally saw how beneficial it was for marketing to partner with sales to help increase revenue. The partnership made sense to me and I wondered why it hadn't been done this way before. I made a direct link between what marketing did for sales and how I could leverage their work to increase my sales to hit quota.

I wasn't the only one to have an "aha" moment. The energy of the room had shifted. All my sales colleagues were engaged and asking real questions on how to best use the tool to help them sell more. Suddenly, we were talking marketing's language. What?! Sales and marketing seemed like one team with one goal that day. We were discussing a marketing resource that could not only help us better manage our time (a salesperson's most precious asset), but how to increase our close rates. This was an overdue conversation we needed to have because it directly benefited our results.

This one presentation changed my entire perspective. The marketing leader took the time to explain how their work was relevant to helping the sales team increase sales.

INTRODUCTION

Why We Need Togetherness

"A single arrow is easily broken, but not ten in a bundle."

— Japanese Proverb

What is togetherness and what does it have to do with aligning sales and marketing teams to accelerate revenue growth?

Sales and marketing misalignment is not a new problem. So why haven't most B2B companies cracked the code on fixing it once and for all? Is it due to management's lack of motivation to do the work needed to transform opaque silos into transparent ones? Perhaps management has not yet realized at the core that misalignment is a people issue.

Fixing misalignment is not easy and requires more than just reorganizing roles, sharing templates, and tweaking processes created under old marketplace conditions. True alignment in the new B2B business takes active leadership and a shared vision with built-in cross-functional trust and incentives for collaboration. With the overwhelming amount of research from top analyst firms and more companies leveraging alignment to achieve better results, leaders should be ready and willing to do whatever it takes to identify the root cause of why misalignment persists in their companies and take the necessary steps to address all underlying issues. Transforming sales and marketing into an aligned, high-performance Revenue Engine does require a significant amount of commitment and change management from leadership, but it can and has been done successfully by leaders willing to take the plunge.

Management wants employees to work together toward a common goal, but they need to acknowledge what motivates and incentivizes employees to initiate collaboration. This is why it was necessary for me to invite experts in psychology, neuroscience, and human collaboration on TheAlignmentPodcast.com. I wanted to ensure we could have a holistic conversation about transformation that covered all necessary viewpoints. This is the only way to come to a solution that works for all involved.

Leaders cannot create and implement cross-functional solutions from the comfort of their opaque silos. Management must have a conversation that includes perspectives from all the departments that influence the buyer's journey. Companies should start with the two most important customer-facing functions: sales and marketing. Once companies create a synergy between these two departments, it will be easier to do the same among the other departments.

In my keynote presentation titled, "Togetherness: Achieving Sales and Marketing Alignment," I refer to sales and marketing like two siblings at a family reunion who are asked to join forces in a three-legged race, but don't realize they must coordinate efforts to finish the race and win. They are focused only on winning as individuals, so they can't see their approach has made it difficult for them.

This book is for all B2B leaders tired of short-sighted tips and tricks that provide short-term, marginal improvements to fix misalignment. In the following chapters, leaders will learn what strategies it takes to build a solid foundation for sales and marketing teams to enjoy a lasting and profitable partnership.

CHAPTER 1

What Makes a Team Successful?

"None of us is as smart as all of us."

– Ken Blanchard

In 2012, Google initiated a two-year study of 180 teams, **Project Aristotle**[1], comprised of Google's most talented employees to unlock the secrets to team effectiveness. The insight resulting from this study is a great example of what company traits are necessary to improve the relationship between sales and marketing so they can operate as one team with increased effectiveness. Google's research found five traits that lead to effective teams:

- Psychological Safety

- Dependability

- Structure and Clarity

- Meaning

- Impact

This groundbreaking research helps identify the key components of creating togetherness between sales and marketing. More often than not, the dysfunction between sales and marketing is due to the relationship not providing its members with one or several of the key traits that Project Aristotle identifies.

---

1   Duhigg, Charles. 2016, February. "What Google Learned From Its Quest to Build the Perfect Team." Retrieved from https://www.nytimes.com/2016/02/28/magazine/what-google-learned-from-its-quest-to-build-the-perfect-team.html

Achieving alignment between sales and marketing goes beyond people, process, and technology, which many solely focus on. This relationship has been strained for a very long time, so leaders will have to build a bridge between these often-estranged teams. They must not only focus on changing the company culture in which sales and marketing operate, but also focus on changing the dynamics between the two teams. When leaders do this, they can create an essence of "we are in this together," "my success is dependent on the success of the team," and "what I do has a direct impact on my team members." While leaders may not want to talk about feelings in a business book, I strongly urge them to seriously consider creating togetherness in their organizations.

Developing a culture that embodies these five elements of togetherness will help improve the relationship between sales and marketing and, ultimately, lead to everyone working together more effectively.

Trust – Members feel safe since their colleagues will always do what is best for the team, rather than follow individual, self-serving motives. To do this, leaders must:

- Solicit input and feedback routinely from both sales and marketing on how things are working.

- Encourage cross-functional work experiences and create sub-teams for special projects.

- Establish transparency in decision-making and communication.

Accountability – Leaders establish clear expectations and hold all team members accountable when goals are not met. To do this, leaders must:

- Focus on demonstrating marketing ROI on programs and campaigns.

- Tie marketing-variable income to revenue targets.

- Share revenue-generation metrics across both teams.

Structure and Clarity – Members are clear on overall team goals, how their work contributes to achieving those goals, and what is expected from them to achieve those goals. To do this, leaders must:

- Create clear goals and objectives, and a path showing how to achieve them.

- Share goals often and reinforce how sales and marketing both directly contribute to helping achieve those goals.

- Establish clear expectations between sales and marketing.

Meaning – Members feel connected to the overall vision of why the team exists. To do this, leaders must:

- Create a shared vision that connects with everyone's hearts and minds.

- Develop a customer-focused company culture.

- Create a "what's best for the customer" mantra.

Impact – Leaders demonstrate how sales and marketing efforts contribute to the team achieving its goals. To do this, leaders must:

- Hold regular cross-functional meetings to highlight the impact of each function's efforts and how these led to achieving revenue goals.

- Share marketing campaign results with sales.

- Openly praise cross-functional collaboration that led to achieving key milestones.

- Create empathy between sales and marketing by encouraging a better understanding of what each team does on a day-to-day basis.

Building a culture focused on these aspects will have a profound effect on the sales and marketing relationship, and ultimately, revenue growth. In a culture of togetherness, both teams will be connected to a common purpose and motivated to place customer needs ahead of individual ones. Creating a feeling of "us" rather than "me" will have a profound effect on the organization's ability to become customer-focused to meet the demands of the modern buyer. If leaders continue to ignore or minimize the sales and marketing misalignment issues, they do so at their own peril and handicap their ability to achieve significant growth.

WHAT DOES MISALIGNMENT LOOK LIKE?

Most B2B organizations have some level of misalignment between sales and marketing, whether leaders admit it or not. What is more shocking is that too many organizations refuse to recognize the problem is as bad as it is. Misalignment slowly destroys a company from the inside out, but it won't be felt until it's too late. Companies can stop the decay by getting an objective perspective to better understand the health of their sales-marketing relationship. Only then can leaders face the detrimental consequences of misalignment and build one of the most powerful tools for company growth – a high-performance Revenue Engine.

In my work as a keynote speaker, consultant, and an executive producer of a fast-growing international podcast, B2B leaders have often asked how to determine whether sales and marketing are misaligned in their organization. Though an in-depth assessment and analysis would need to be conducted to understand the dynamics in play, the following are some telltale signs to look for. If one or several of these issues exist within a company, it's time to get serious about alignment.

Key Indicators of Sales and Marketing Misalignment:

- Marketing-generated leads produce low- or no-close rates.

- Combative or dysfunctional relationships exist between sales and marketing leaders.

- Marketing takes no responsibility or accountability for revenue contribution.

- Sales and marketing use different data to evaluate business performance.

- Sales and Marketing tell two different or conflicting stories about business performance.

- Customers complain about a poor customer experience or the difficulties of purchasing from the company.

- Sales and Marketing disagree on target customers and the unique value proposition of the company.

- Sales and Marketing don't share their insights or business intelligence.

- Sales and/or Marketing leaders often complain about misalignment.

The B2B economy is in the midst of a seismic shift due to digital disruption. The buyer is coming to the conversation with more information than ever before. Dave Elkington, founder of InsideSales. com, addressed the issue on TheAlignmentPodcast.com, Ep. 39. According to Elkington, there is a massive amount of information inequality between buyers and sellers. Today's buyers have access to deep research. They have been on the company website, talked with their peers, and have done all of that before they even engage with a sales rep. Because buyers have access to a nearly unlimited amount of information, limiting conversations to product and service features and benefits is not enough to satisfy them. Organizations must provide the valuable, personalized insights that buyers are demanding, and sales and marketing must join forces as one unified team to meet those demands.

Winners and losers are being created in today's marketplace. Company leaders must decide whether to be proactive by setting up their company for success in the new B2B economy, or wait until it's too late to take action. Leaders who choose to wait will find that when they are ready to take action, they will be at such a stark disadvantage that becoming competitive will feel like an unsurmountable task.

Leaders, the choice is yours.

For those who are ready, let's start the journey to creating togetherness.

CHAPTER 2

The Cost of Misalignment

"There are risks and cost to action. But they are far less than the long-range risks of comfortable inaction."

– John F. Kennedy

Misalignment costs much more than leaders think. It's estimated that "lost sales productivity and wasted marketing budget cost companies at least $1 trillion a year."[2] To put that in perspective, someone with $1 trillion could buy Apple, Inc., outright, or perhaps, the country of Switzerland, if it were for sale.

According to InsideSales.com[3], sales reps spend only 36.6% of their time on selling. In addition, Marketo and Reachforce[4] show us that sales reps ignore 80 percent of marketing-generated leads. Looking at the facts in this manner makes it easier to understand how the sales and marketing teams of a company can be working hard, but not leveraging each other in the best or most efficient way, and thus not able to achieve the revenue growth the company desires. International Data Corporation (IDC) puts things into even easier terms to grasp by showing that a company's misalignment of sales and marketing technologies and processes costs them approximately 10 percent or more of annual revenue.

---

2   Marketo and Reachforce: *101 B2B Marketing and Sales Tips from The B2B Lead*
3   Larsen, Gabe. 2017, November. "Sales Reps Only Spend 36.6% of Time Actually Selling." Retrieved from https://blog.insidesales.com/research/time-management-for-sales-reps/
4   Marketo and Reachforce: *101 B2B Marketing and Sales Tips from The B2B Lead.*

Thus, a $250M company could lose upwards of $25M in annual revenue due to a dysfunctional relationship between sales and marketing. With this perspective, it is clear that alignment is about much more than just getting along; it is about the company's ability to achieve revenue growth. Even if leaders were able to save the organization just 1 percent of lost revenue due to misalignment ($250,000 – the equivalent of one or two executive salaries), wouldn't the effort be worth it?

> **TheAlignmentPodcast.com**
> **Episode 20 | AI Increases Sales Productivity**
>
> "Some of your best-paid people who impact the whole health of the company are now spending over half of their time not selling but doing administrative tasks that we somehow need in the back office. That's wrong."
>
> **– Stefan Groschupf,**
> Founder and CEO of Automation Hero

Most sales leaders would agree that time is a sales representative's most valuable asset. The environment in which leaders are currently asking salespeople to operate robs them of this very asset and is one reason many struggle to hit quota. Why do, on average, only 54.3 percent of B2B sales reps achieve their quota?[5] Stats like these demonstrate that sales leaders are failing to empower their sales representatives to achieve their goals. Leaders must invest in the tools and resources that their sales teams need to be able to thrive in the modern selling environment.

The knee-jerk reaction for many leaders is to hire more sales reps to hit their pipeline coverage target and increase the probability of hitting company quotas. Instead, leaders would benefit from taking a more thoughtful approach, as an increase in the number of sales reps on the team does not equate to increased sales productivity.

---

5   CSO Insights. 2019. "Selling in the Age of Ceaseless Change: The 2018-2019 Sales Performance Report." Retrieved from https://www.csoinsights.com/wp-content/up-loads/sites/5/2018/12/2018-2019-Sales-Performance-Report.pdf

Sales productivity involves two factors – efficiency and effectiveness. Hiring more sales reps does not help to bolster either of those factors.

Pipeline coverage can be influenced by three leverages – quantity, velocity, and quality.[6] Most companies focus primarily on quantity of deals inside the pipeline and disregard the other two levers. With the B2B selling environment becoming more complex every day, focusing solely on quantity is short-sighted and problematic. Leaders should take a more holistic approach to pipeline coverage to determine how they will increase pipeline quality and sales velocity. Evidence continually shows that the most efficient way to achieve such success is through aligning sales and marketing.

Misalignment, for most companies, is like being in a leaking rowboat with no oars in the middle of a lake. Everyone knows a hole exists as they take on water, but as long as they are able to scoop the water out of the boat, then everyone is okay. This results in allowing a change in focus – quickly getting the water out of the boat instead of finding a way to permanently plug the hole.

It's not until the boat takes on too much water or loses its buoyancy that those inside the boat realize the situation is much more serious. In a company losing revenue in this way, the problem has become so pervasive the company must either take drastic action to move in a different direction or its employees will bail out and find a better employer.

Beyond misalignment's negative impact on the company's ability to effectively drive revenue growth, it adversely affects the culture of the organization. Consider some of the effects of misalignment:

---

6   Bauer, Emily. 2017, May. "What Does Your Sales Pipeline Coverage Ratio Reveal About Your Business?" Retrieved from https://www.propellercrm.com/blog/sales-pipeline-coverage

MISTRUST

Misalignment breeds mistrust because teams tend to have different goals with competing agendas. This can cause team members to hoard information to stack the deck in their own favor to achieve goals. Business intelligence and customer insights are important competitive advantages. When team members' lack of trust causes them to withhold information, it places the entire organization at risk. It can also cause the company to miss out on significant opportunities and changes in customer preferences and market dynamics.

The lack of sharing information also leads to redundant work that wastes time, money, and resources – another example of lost productivity.

BAD CUSTOMER EXPERIENCE

Customer Experience (CX) has become more important than ever before. For many buyers, CX is more important than price or product. This means buyers will be willing to pay more for a potentially inferior product or one that might not meet 100% of their needs.

Consider how Amazon has changed customer expectations. Everyone now has the ability to access all product information online, read customer reviews, and quickly make purchases. The process is quick, easy, and seamless. This ability to make a purchasing decision with ease has crept into buyers' expectations when making professional purchasing decisions. Today's modern buyers expect a seamless buying experience, much like what they are used to outside of the office in their personal lives. They are not concerned about whether the information is coming from marketing or sales. They just want it delivered in a timely manner and relevant to their unique priorities.

LACK OF STRATEGIC CLARITY

Misalignment can cause individuals to become frustrated by not knowing what to focus on. This inability to focus is a hit to productivity and motivation when people don't know where to place their energy and efforts. They then tend to spread themselves too thin by trying to do everything, which results in mediocre results and burnout.

Many companies are unsure of who their target customers are; as a result, they go after several types or try to reach everyone. When this occurs, marketing cannot provide adequate support for sales to initiate productive conversations with the right buyers. This further results in the sales team finding no value in the content and resources marketing produces, and marketing becomes frustrated about wasting their time producing resources that are not seen as helpful.

There is both an economic and cultural cost to the organization in allowing misalignment to exist[7]. When leaders look to quantify the cost of misalignment, they cannot overlook its significant impact on creating an environment of mistrust, frustration, confusion, and lost motivation. These factors lead to people leaving the organization or staying in their jobs doing the bare minimum, which again has a direct economic impact on the company. In the end, misalignment is extremely costly for any-sized organization.

HOW MISALIGNED ARE SALES AND MARKETING?

Determining the level of misalignment between the sales and marketing teams is difficult without an objective point of view. Visit the URL below for a quick assessment of how aligned your teams are. This tool is based on past client interactions, respected research, and professional experience."

www.TheAlignmentTest.com

---

7   Kotler, P., Rackham, N., & Krishnaswamy, Suj. 2006, July-August. "End the War Between Sales and Marketing." Retrieved from https://hbr.org/2006/07/ending-the-war-between-sales-and-marketing

CHAPTER 3

Alignment: The Revenue Generator

"If you want to go fast, go alone. If you want to go far, go together."

— **African Proverb**

For leaders who may think sales and marketing alignment is just a buzzword, management fad, or terminology to add to your business lingo, let me be clear – alignment is about revenue growth. It is imperative for all B2B leaders to understand that not taking action to align their teams will have a negative impact on their company's ability to compete with forward-thinking leaders who have already recognized the changing dynamics of the vendor-buyer relationship. Alignment is not about two departments getting along. It is about establishing an internal relationship that ensures the organization's ability to effectively connect with buyers to win their business – thus driving revenue growth for the organization.

A compelling study titled "Marketing/Sales Alignment 2016: Who Is Agile Enough To Win?"[8] was conducted by Aberdeen Group and showed a direct link between alignment and improvement in critical business outcomes.

---

8   Ostrow, Peter. 2016, March. "Marketing/Sales Alignment 2016: Who Is Agile Enough to Win?" www.Aberdeen.com

Why Alignment is Worth the Effort

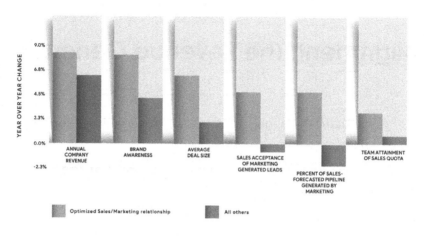

Figure 1: Aberdeen Group shows how companies with aligned sales and marketing teams outperform their competitors.
Source: Ostrow, Peter. 2016, March. "Marketing/Sales Alignment 2016: Who Is Agile Enough to Win?" www.Aberdeen.com

The study produced significant insights that remain relevant today. One pivotal question the study addressed was, "How Do I Know If All This Effort is Worthwhile?" Sales and marketing leaders, as well as CEOs, ask themselves the same question today. "Yes" is the answer, and here's why.

The study found companies with highly aligned sales and marketing teams vastly outperformed their competitors in revenue growth and other key business metrics.

The business metrics included:

- Annual company revenue.

- Brand awareness.

- Average deal size.

- Sales acceptance of marketing-generated leads.

- Percent of sales-forecasted pipeline generated by marketing.

- Team attainment of sales quota.

Although, some may think research doesn't always represent actual business performance, the story that these results illustrate cannot be ignored. After a deeper review of these findings, two key themes emerge that should raise concern for any B2B leader:

- There is a direct and significant link between alignment and some of the key drivers of revenue growth.

- There is a drastic and notable difference in company performance between aligned companies and those not aligned.

The Aberdeen Group study clearly demonstrates that alignment not only helps the company increase revenue, but helps it compete in a unique way that cannot easily be duplicated.

ALIGNMENT HAS BECOME A COMPETITIVE ADVANTAGE

Beyond all the metrics that show alignment's positive impact on revenue growth, leaders need to start looking at alignment as a competitive advantage – because it is. Alignment puts an organization in a position where it is able to provide the modern buyer with value that a misaligned organization cannot. Considering alignment as a competitive advantage is especially important for company leaders who run organizations in highly competitive industries where there are a significant number of competitors. Alignment is an advantage that cannot easily be replicated nor achieved overnight. These facts all reinforce that company leaders should treat alignment transformation as a strategic priority. Listed are the competitive advantages that alignment provides.

1. More Efficient Revenue Growth

Not all growth is created equal. Many B2B companies continue to approach the market as they always have and seem perplexed about why their revenue growth has stalled or declined. They have not realized that the "spray and pray" method used in days gone by is no longer effective. While you may be able to make gains in growth by the sheer volume of the resources you throw at the wall, it is an outdated strategy that is unsustainable and produces a ton of waste and lost productivity. This significant waste eats at the revenue that is generated by sales and marketing, and is the reason the misaligned company is able only to generate minimal or no new revenue gains.

Today's successful B2B organization is more strategic and agile with their approach. They are laser-focused and play where they can win. This focus allows the organization to be able to tell what is and is not working and to pivot quickly to change how they are approaching the market. Revenue leaders in the aligned organization also have a different mindset about how they evaluate performance. In this new, complex B2B landscape, purely looking at volume is not advised (e.g. more leads, more demos, more clicks, bigger mailing list). This change in mindset means that marketing leaders are willing to have the uncomfortable conversation with their sales counterpart that the number of leads they are providing may go down.[9] And that's okay. If sales leaders want marketing to focus on attracting better-quality opportunities, they must be ready to sacrifice the number of leads their team receives. However, with a clearer understanding of the types of accounts that have the highest chances of actually becoming customers, sales leaders will see an increase in conversion rates. This focus on quality over volume helps remove some of the financial burden of additional sales headcount and marketing spend, thus allowing the company to drive revenue in a more efficient manner and outperform their less aligned competitors.

2. Clearer Understanding of the Buyer

The company that best understands the buyer wins. Aligned sales and marketing organizations have the advantage of being able to tap into the tribal knowledge of everyone. The ability to access this tribal knowledge not only provides access to critical customer and market intelligence, it also allows the company to anticipate and

---

9   Davis, Jeff. 2019, April. "Want to Know How to Build a Quality Sales Pipeline?" Retrieved from https://blog.sellingpower.com/gg/2019/04/want-to-know-how-to-build-a-quality-sales-pipeline.html

react faster to changing customer and market dynamics than their competitors. This collective knowledge and close collaboration also enable the company to get more precise in understand the finer details of their target buyers. This specificity enables the company to improve customer targeting and truly provide personalized buyer interactions that create intimacy and trust.

3. Enhanced Customer Experience (CX)

CX can be a challenging concept for leaders to wrap their heads around, but without a doubt, it strongly influences the modern buyer's willingness to buy from a company. Nothing will cause a buyer to stop engaging with a company faster than an irrelevant or bad interaction with sales or marketing that adds no value to help them complete the tasks they deem necessary before making an informed buying decision that is best for them. Buyers are so overwhelmed with information that many buying teams are unable to even make a buying decision. This is the paradox of choice. Barry Schwartz, an American psychologist, introduced the concept of the paradox of choice in his book, *The Paradox of Choice* (2005) and argues that offering more choice creates a psychological burden (e.g. stress, anxiety, frustration) that can turn consumers off. More choice means more time and effort expended in choosing and increased odds that the consumer will make the wrong choice and regret it. This is exactly what the average B2B buyer is going through and why buyers are choosing to spend money with companies that make the buying experience as easy as possible – even if the company's product is more expensive or inferior in quality.

4. More Valuable Revenue Pipeline

Aligned sales and marketing teams benefit from a higher quality pipeline because they have a clearer picture of who their ideal customers are, and both sales and marketing contribute to building that pipeline. While a company may have more pipeline coverage, a misaligned sales and marketing team may cause that pipeline to be of less value because the conversion rate on the majority of deals is so low. In essence, an aligned company's pipeline could be of more economic value even if the total revenue potential is less because its conversion potential is higher. This is the power of quality over quantity.

> **TheAlignmentPodcast.com**
> **Episode 19 | Marketing Must Help Sales Eliminate Bad Leads**
>
> "What we have to make sure of is that marketing, in their lead generation process…is aligned with who the target prospect is. It's not just a name. It's not just an email. It's much more than that."
>
> – *Mark Hunter,*
> keynote sales speaker and best-selling author, *High Profit Prospecting*

HOW SALES AND MARKETING LEADERS BENEFIT EACH OTHER

Alignment starts at the top. Even though the company will need all leaders to be on board to make an alignment transformation a success, the sales and marketing leaders must inspect the health of their relationship very early in the process. An organization cannot expect to fix a dysfunctional relationship between the sales and marketing teams if their leaders have a conflicting or nonexistent relationship.

I delivered the opening keynote at the annual TMSA (Transportation Marketing and Sales Association) conference about the power of partnerships. After leaving the stage, a sales leader explained that my presentation opened his eyes to the fact that he should be working with his marketing counterpart in a much different way, but he had been a "sales guy" his entire career. And, even though he and his marketing colleague got along fine, he had no idea what marketing did or how he would even start to work with them in a different way. This is a perfect example of two leaders who got along in a social context but didn't see how their departments could connect to work together to increase revenue. Neither one saw the benefits of aligning their department's work to increase the overall success of each team.

Many sales and marketing leaders I have worked with suffer from this same dilemma – a willingness to work together, but no knowledge of how to do so. Thus, it is important that sales and marketing leaders be more informed about how to effectively leverage each other so they can build a stronger business relationship and help each other achieve their goals.

To help leaders who are unsure of how their counterpart can help them be more effective at achieving their goals, listed below are some of the best ways sales and marketing leaders can leverage each other to be more successful.

The top benefits marketing leaders can offer sales leaders are:[10]

- Support in targeting the best types of accounts and opportunities.

- Increasing brand awareness with the right types of accounts.

- Providing educational events that bring customers and target buyers together to learn and share experiences.

- Creating tools that help sales present their solution to target buyers in a way that clearly demonstrates the value it provides and is in the buyer's language.

- Customer and buyer insights.

- Information on macro-level trends to be able to position sales reps as trusted advisors.

---

10   Ramos, Laura. 2015, March. "From Priming the Pipeline to Engaging Buyers: The B2B CMO's New Role in Sales Enablement." www.forrester.com

The top benefits sales leaders can offer marketing leaders are:

- A continuous focus on achieving revenue targets.

- Voice of the customer feedback and competitive intelligence.

- Help tying marketing campaigns and programs to closed deals to evaluate marketing ROI.

- Clarity on what sales representatives need to be successful.

- Ensuring content speaks to customers in their language, not marketing-speak.

- Guidance on the sales team's ability to execute on marketing programs.

Increasing the sales and marketing leaders' understanding of how they can directly benefit each other provides them a starting point to have a real conversation about working together in a different way. When these leaders are empowered to ask for what they need explicitly from each other rather than complain that the other isn't doing their job, real progress can be made in building a true collaborative relationship between the sales and marketing leader as well as their teams.

CHAPTER 4

The Origins of Misalignment

"Not everything that is faced can be changed. But nothing can be changed until it is faced."

— James Baldwin

A nagging question on this journey is — did sales and marketing ever get along? What caused the change in how management treated the two functions, which caused the change in how they viewed each other?

To discuss the dysfunctional relationship between sales and marketing without understanding how it started will not allow us to develop solutions that address the problem at hand. Without this knowledge, companies would be guessing at the issue and developing short-term fixes directed at the symptoms rather than the problem itself.

THE ORIGINS OF MARKETING

Marketing, as it is known today, began as a function of Sales.[11] The Industrial Revolution (1760–1840) gave birth to the concept of marketing. This time of rapid industrial innovation enabled companies to mass produce products, which then made it easier for consumers to purchase goods rather than produce them themselves. In conjunction with the country's improving transportation infrastructure, mass media also became more prevalent. These forces came together to create rapidly growing consumer desires for new

---

11   Hardy, James. 2016, September. "The History of Marketing: From Trade to Tech." Retrieved from https://historycooperative.org/the-evolution-of-marketing-from-trade-to-tech/

products and the need for manufacturers to find more comprehensive ways to inform customers that these new products existed. Thus, the marketing function was born.

As competition between manufacturers intensified in the early 20th century, they had to find ways to create preferences in the mind of consumers to offset similar product offerings by competing companies. This was the emergence of branding. By the 1960s, many industries were so challenged by the competition that specific skills in direct marketing were needed. Due to fierce competition in the marketplace, marketing departments began to appear in every company. As this function grew, so did its influence within the corporate hierarchy. Marketing became involved in strategic planning and the department's input was sought for pricing strategy, innovative communication methods, pinpointing the ideal customer, and more. The increasing influence and importance of the marketing department began the divide and misalignment experienced by sales and marketing. As marketing was considered to be a more strategic function, a greater divide emerged between the two, having far-reaching effects on B2B companies.

Over time, marketing evolved into a discipline with significant clout within the company. Up to the mid-1950s, the term marketing was generally synonymous with sales. The focus was on selling product instead of valuing or meeting consumers' needs.[12]

FOUR TYPES OF SALES-MARKETING CONFIGURATIONS

Sales and marketing teams are not organized the same way in many different companies. Organization is influenced by many factors, such as company size, departmental leadership, CEO level of functional expertise, complexity of product offering, and more.

In *Improving Sales and Marketing Collaboration: A Step-by-Step Guide* by Avinash Malshe, Ph.D. and Wim Biemans, Ph.D., it is

---

12   Webster, F.E. 1988. "The Rediscovery of the Marketing Concept." *Business Horizons.* (May-June), 1988. p. 31.

shown that the quality of the relationship between sales and marketing strongly depends on how the two teams are configured within the organization. Through their extensive research, they found the sales-marketing interface typically falls into one of four categories. These four categories represent a spectrum of the increasing maturity of the sales-marketing relationship. By examining the company's sales-marketing configuration, leaders can be more intentional in making necessary changes to transform the two teams into better alignment. There may be structural and/or cultural issues needing to be addressed before beginning the alignment transformation journey.

Four Sales-Marketing Configurations

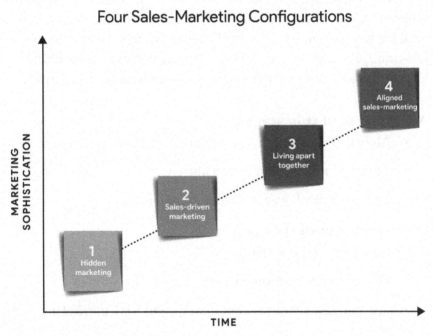

Figure 2: Four sales-marketing configurations.
Source: Malshe, Avinash and Biemans, Wim, "Improving Sales and Marketing Collaboration: A Step-by-Step Guide" (2015)

HIDDEN MARKETING

B2B companies falling into the hidden marketing category lack a formal marketing department, and the activities that would typically be covered by a marketing professional (e.g. development of the ICP (ideal customer profile), market positioning, sales collateral, etc.) are performed ad-hoc by the CEO or sales leader. Thus, marketing is "hidden" throughout the roles and responsibilities of leaders in the organization. Companies at this stage tend to be small and have a short-term focus on closing deals. "These companies either fail to appreciate how a separate marketing function and a more strategic perspective may improve performance or they are simply too small for a dedicated marketing manager." (Malshe and Biemans)

With no dedicated marketing manager, leaders must first recognize the benefits of taking a more strategic approach to their activities. This will help them become more efficient in targeting the right types of buyers, thereby increasing win rates and building a more scalable foundation for growth. This can be achieved by adding a full-time, part-time, or freelance marketing manager, or by both the CEO and sales leader developing long-term marketing strategies.

Advantages of this stage:

- Ability to highly focus on individual customer needs

- Ability to make changes quickly

- Tighter control over customer experiences

Disadvantages of this stage:

- Lack of strategic clarity

- Always in fire-fighting mode

- Ignores the revenue-generating potential marketing can provide

SALES-DRIVEN MARKETING

This stage represents companies that have grown to where sales now needs a support function, which company leaders deem should be a marketing team. Key duties for marketing teams in this configuration include day-to-day sales activities that sales may not have the time to do (i.e. sales collateral, registering the company for trade shows, creating branded swag for customers, etc.). In this configuration, sales has sole responsibility for the relationship with the customer and is generally not open to sharing detailed account information for fear of marketing over-stepping its power and communicating directly with the customer. This can be seen as undermining the authority of the sales representative inside the account. Marketing managers may develop strategic marketing, but leadership will give priority to sales or customer-related activities because the plans are not considered to directly impact increasing revenue.

Advantages of sales-driven marketing stage:
- Sales has a support function to allow them to dedicate more time to sales-related activities.

- Marketing allows the company to be more aware of marketplace and customer trends.

- Company can deliver marketing activities (e.g. events, direct mail, branded sales presentations, etc.) that sales may not have the expertise in or time to execute.

Disadvantages of this stage:
- Company leaders don't fully understand marketing's value.

- Sales may withhold key information from marketing, not allowing them to make the most impactful decision for the organization.

- Marketing has little to no relationship with the customer.

LIVING APART TOGETHER

In this stage, companies have distinct sales and marketing functions. Individuals within each function have specific experience and expertise allowing them to meet the demands of their job description. Having a more mature marketing function allows these companies to tackle more strategic issues. While instances exist where sales and marketing may collaborate, for example on closing a large key account, this is not usually the case. Sales and marketing typically exist and operate in separate silos. Thus, living apart together.

They rarely exchange information on company performance as it relates to closing deals with new customers. There is no established feedback loop to help both teams improve their approach with potential customers. This translates to marketing creating plans, programs, and campaigns in a vacuum. These plans may fail to resonate with the sales team because marketing has not taken into account changing market dynamics, customers' true needs, the competition, or sales' ability to execute on the plan. This lack of awareness causes sales to question if marketing "gets it," and sales not valuing the work marketing produces or completely ignoring the plans. Adoption of CRM also tends to be low unless strictly enforced by sales management.

Advantages of this stage:
- Focus shifts toward more strategic goals and objectives.
- Marketing shares business intelligence across the entire organization.
- A company brand can be established and built.

Disadvantages of this stage:
- Turf war occurs between sales and marketing.
- Challenge emerges to adopt a customer-focused approach.
- Marketing receives little to no feedback on effectiveness of strategies in closing new business, and struggles to determine marketing ROI.
- Sales is unable to properly leverage marketing output to help with time management and efficiency.
- Company struggles to improve targeting based on won or lost deals.

ALIGNED SALES-MARKETING

Companies in this group have separate sales and marketing functions that are jointly responsible for marketing plans and programs. Marketing leaders actively seek input from sales leaders to co-create marketing plans that leverage each team's strengths. Marketing also stays in lock-step with sales as they execute marketing plans to ensure success and to assess the effectiveness of different strategies. This level of alignment is realized through formal meetings and communications. There is a feedback loop put in place to ensure each team is continuously learning from the other and altering activities if necessary.

When sales and marketing have equal stakes in the success of plans and strategies, they are incentivized to share innovative ideas and critical feedback. "The free flow of information, combined with mutual respect, facilitate collaboration in almost all sales and marketing activities, such as identifying new market opportunities, creating new product offerings and responding to changes in the marketplace. Both sales and marketing view collaboration as essential to their day-to-day work." (Malshe and Biemans)

Advantages of this stage:
- Company can be highly customer-focused and deliver seamless CX.

- Incentives are aligned with better collaboration.

- Formalized, continuous communication enables company to become a learning organization that can quickly adapt to changing buyer and/or customer needs.

Disadvantages of this stage:
- Groupthink can set in as team members develop strong interpersonal relationships.

- Consensus-driven decision making may delay the process of taking action.

- An increased number of cross-functional stakeholders must be included as plans are being developed.

Leaders can use this framework to get clarity on the sales-marketing configuration currently being used in their organization. This insight gives leaders a chance to see if pursuing an alignment transformation makes sense in the current conditions of their organization. Going from a sales-driven marketing stage to an aligned sales-marketing stage takes tremendous effort and may ultimately fail because the transition is not only for the sales and marketing teams, but everyone in the organization.

The progressing stages of the sales-marketing configuration continuum takes a considerable amount of change in company structure and culture. It's recommended to first establish a "Living Apart Together" sales-marketing configuration, then pursue an alignment transformation.

As senior leadership support and influence of the marketing team increases through the sales-marketing configuration stages, several sources of tension may arise. Leaders need to be aware of these potential tensions so they can proactively manage them and provide a smoother path to achieving increased alignment between sales and marketing.

TRANSFORMING MARKETING TO A PROFIT CENTER FROM A COST CENTER

Marketing historically has operated as a cost center. A cost center can be defined as a department within an organization that does not directly add to profit, but still costs the organization money to operate. Cost centers indirectly contribute to a company's profitability. Marketing was allowed to operate in this capacity without question, as they were never asked to demonstrate a direct contribution to revenue growth or report on their marketing program's ROI. Until recently, leaders saw the department as a price that had to be paid in order to sell products and services. Leaders now understand they must look more closely at the cost of revenue generation and realize marketing activities play a significant role in that cost. Like any cost in the organization, marketing expenses should be considered in the context of how much revenue it generates. When marketing is treated as a cost center, they have little to no incentive to ensure they monitor the results produced. The greater focus is on spending the entire allocated budget given by upper management. This spending ensures receiving at least the same if not greater amount next year. This treatment creates a "use it or lose it" mindset for marketing leaders. It also frustrates sales reps, as they think marketing projects are created to justify marketing salaries, which in fact many times is indeed the case.

LEARNING TO SPEAK THE SAME LANGUAGE

Differences in department lingo can create significant communication confusion and tension between these two groups. Marketing-speak and sales-speak within each group doesn't cause concern, but it does cause problems when introducing cross-functional interactions. During the most recent Sales + Marketing Alignment SummitTM, an educational event series I created exclusively for senior-level B2B sales and marketing leaders, a vice president of inside sales at a large telecommunications company served as a panelist. He shared an example of how two teams argued over the same issue using different definitions and neither understood what the other was saying. It ended up that the team wasted 45 mins because of ineffective communication and lack of defining the problem to begin with. Serious breakdowns in communication cause frustration, erode confidence in others, and are detrimental to successful work relationships.

As sales and marketing teams meet regularly and discuss the pipeline, leaders must agree on the definitions, terminology, and metrics of the revenue funnel. Neither side benefits from using jargon or terminology not easily understood by the other group. What is a MQL (marketing qualified lead)? What is a lead? When does the sales cycle start? What is the lead-scoring methodology? These are the types of discussions to conduct early on and often to ensure clarity when working together.

SYNCING DIFFERENT TIMELINES

Sales and marketing experience time differently, which causes a disconnect in the sense of urgency. Marketing routinely develops plans two to three quarters ahead to ensure enough time is allowed for execution. Sales, on the other hand, is focused on closing deals to hit quarterly quotas. When sales asks marketing for an ad-hoc sales piece or program to help close a deal, and marketing says they can't due to budget or resource restraints, sales knows marketing doesn't share their sense of urgency. Though both are focused on the customer, their time horizons are different.

Frequent cross-functional meetings allow marketing to understand what is the top priority for sales, and allows marketing to share long-term plans in bite-sized pieces so sales understands how those plans will affect them in the immediate future. These meetings will alleviate the discord in priorities between the two teams.

LEVERAGING DIFFERENT TYPES OF KNOWLEDGE

Today, most marketing positions require a marketing degree. There was no degree in professional sales available to help in pursuing a sales career until recently. Most salespeople got their education on the job. Because of this, many sales managers didn't see the benefit of obtaining an advanced degree as it didn't guarantee a promotion to sales leader nor the opportunity to make more money.

Marketing managers, on the other hand, tend to obtain advanced degrees since they are rewarded with higher salaries and senior-level titles. This difference in intrinsic value to a company creates an image that marketers have knowledge superior to those in sales. This creates an intellectual hierarchy between sales and marketing, which adds to the separation and inequality of the two. To succeed in connecting with the modern buyer, companies need both teams to have an equal mix of educational knowledge and people savvy.

A number of universities have recognized the need for a formal sales program due to the increasing complexity of the B2B selling environment. Some of the top universities offering professional selling programs now include institutions such as:[13]

- Northern Illinois University – College of Business, Professional Sales Program led by Professor Robert Peterson, Ph.D., Dean's Distinguished Professor of Sales

- The University of Texas at Dallas – Naveen Jindal School of Management, Center for Professional Sales led by Professor Howard Dover, Ph.D., Clinical Professor of Marketing

- Baylor University – Hankamer School of Business, Center for Professional Selling led by Andrea Dixon, Ph.D., Associate Professor of Marketing

---

TheAlignmentPodcast.com
Episode 08 | Customer Experience Is The Future Of B2B

"Companies that have historically operated in silos where you've got the marketing organization over here and the sales organization over there are starting to feel the fury of people that understand what a great technology experience can be like and they're now raising their hands and saying enough already. Figure it out."

— Justin Shriber,
VP of Marketing, LinkedIn Sales and Marketing Solutions

WORKING ACROSS SILOS

Companies have supported working in silos for decades. According to PwC's 2015 Global Operations Survey,[14] it is estimated that just more than 55 percent of companies operate in silos. Silos themselves are not the problem for today's communication issues; silo mentality is.

---

13 Sales Education Foundation. 2018. "2018 SEF Top Universities for Professional Sales Education." *Sales Education Annual.* Retrieved from https://salesfoundation. org/wp-content/uploads/2018/04/SEF1801-2018-Annual-Magazine_FINAL_DigitalDownload.pdf"

14 PwC. (2015, October 2015. "PwC's 2015 Global Operations Survey." Retrieved from http://operationssurvey.pwc.com/PwC-2015-Global-Operations-Survey.pdf

Organizational silos, if properly managed, serve a purpose to the company and the teams. Silos allow the company and its employees to develop expertise in a certain area and allow for faster execution of tasks once a cross-departmental decision has been made. Silos were established to create stability but do not address the modern company's need to be flexible and ready to evolve. Leadership must be clear on setting a vision so they can properly manage interactions across silos (teams) to collectively achieve the company's goals.

Leaders should fight the silo mentality, which reduces the efficiency of achieving growth, morale, trust, collaboration, and company culture. Leaders must encourage a shift from "me" to "we" so all employee embrace being a part of one revenue-producing team.

CUSTOMER EXPERIENCE IS EVERYTHING

Walker's "Customers 2020: The Future Of B-To-B Customer Experience" report shows that by 2020, the Customer Experience (CX) will be more important to customers than price or product. In fact, large companies such as Oracle have already created entire business units and even a conference dedicated to addressing this competitive advantage to ensure they are providing the modern buyer a positive and seamless experience. It's impossible to provide a seamless and cohesive CX if teams aren't aligned. What do successful companies have that make working with them easy? People made companies such as Amazon, Costco, Zappos, and Netflix successful because they provide a seamless experience where CX is of the utmost importance.

THE BENEFITS OF CROSS-FUNCTIONAL RELATIONSHIPS

Internal coordination is required to create a cohesive experience for the modern buyer. The necessary tasks aren't restricted to sales and marketing alone. There are a number of departments that have a significant impact on customer experience such as customer success, finance, legal, etc. Strong cross-functional relationships with these other departments are needed to coordinate working with buyers and customers in a cohesive manner. Having these relationships allows teams to obtain the information needed for immediate decisions and ensures many viewpoints are considered when choosing what's best for the customer. These types of relationships enable colleagues to better understand how each department interacts with customers during their journey, as well as which stakeholders should be involved with the various projects and initiatives to successfully execute them.

ENDING THE US VS. THEM

When leaders see their teams talking more about what the other team isn't doing rather than how they can improve delivery to the customer an "Us" versus "Them" relationship develops.[15] Team members see their contribution to the business as a zero-sum game, where they are reluctant to collaborate with others, fearing the other team's success will be their demise. This type of thinking is detrimental to the information flow between teams and can slow the ability to react to changing market forces. This mindset also appears when the company culture allows for a lack of accountability and/or discourages experimentation.

COMMUNICATION AVOIDS DUPLICATION

Silos can create an environment where team efforts are unnecessarily duplicated. This is an inefficient use of time and energy and is costly to the company and demoralizing to the employees. All this can be avoided through clear and transparent communication between teams; they need to know who is working on what to avoid a duplication of efforts.

TRANSFORMING OPAQUE SILOS INTO TRANSPARENT

To combat the silo mentality, leaders must create transparent silos[16] and not allow isolation, which stops information from flowing. Working in isolated silos can cause the teams to miss a critical

15   Ismail, Kaya. 2018, January. "5 Signs Your Organization Is Too Siloed." Retrieved from https://www.cmswire.com/leadership/5-signs-your-organization-is-too-siloed/
16   Novkov, Alexander. 2016, July. "Don't Break Your Silos - Push Out the Silo Mentality." Retrieved from https://www.infoq.com/articles/break-silos-ventilators/

change in the market or dynamic shift in a customer relationship. While everyone enjoys personal privacy, no one would want to live in a house with no windows. They would cut themselves off from important information that might threaten their existence. This is what operating in opaque silos is like.

Developing transparent silos is not an easy task, but when leaders invest the time and energy to ensure the silos have free-flowing communication channels, it can be done.

Some ways in which leaders can fight against opaque silos are by:

- Making sure vision is shared and recognized by all leadership, teams, and colleagues.

- Communicating the vision at least seven times, according to the Marketing Rule of 7. The maxim developed by the movie industry in the 1930s states that someone needs to hear a message at least seven times before they will take action. Leaders should also use multiple communication channels so everyone can internalize the vision (e.g. town hall meetings, newsletters, sales kickoff meetings, and more).

- Measuring and reporting the progress made toward that vision to keep people engaged in achieving success.

- Increasing information flow by scheduling regular cross-departmental meetings.

- Establishing short-term or long-term cross-functional teams to tackle specific tasks or projects.

- Focusing on creating the best Customer Experience (CX) possible.

CHAPTER 5

The Modern Buyer-Seller Relationship

"The greatest danger in times of turbulence is not the turbulence — it is to act with yesterday's logic."

– Peter Drucker

Why has there been so much buzz about sales and marketing alignment lately? The relationship has been dysfunctional for decades, so why must leaders transform their organizations now?

After years of accepting the status quo, companies have no choice but to align sales and marketing to remain competitive. Digital disruption has empowered buyers with nearly unlimited access to information, and they are choosing to extensively self-educate before interacting with the company directly. This means the traditional sales and marketing strategies are becoming less effective. In fact, multiple studies have shown that buyers are already more than halfway through their buying journey before even choosing to interact with a salesperson. As a response to buyers changing the way they buy, sellers must change the way they sell. Just as the internet has disrupted industries like retail, car buying, taxi service, cable TV, and more, it is now disrupting the way B2B buyers buy. The only way leaders can discover a new and more effective approach to marketing and selling is to intimately understand the modern buyer.

INFORMATION INEQUALITY

The result of this digital disruption with the most significant impact is the increased access to information that buyers now have. Digital disruption has given modern buyers access to a nearly unlimited amount of information. This, coupled with increased connectivity to other professionals via social media platforms such as LinkedIn, has placed sales reps at a significant disadvantage in typical sales interactions.

Unless the company has invested in a significant amount of business intelligence tools to provide sales representatives with account and buyer insights, they know very little compared to what the buyer knows. The representative may have basic information like the company name, title, email address, industry size, and annual revenue. These are not deep buyer insights. On the other hand, the buyer has most likely researched a multitude of resources before connecting with the sales representative, including the company website, third-party product review sites, company review sites, professional network connections, and more. Who do you think is more informed coming into this interaction?

This is the reason sales representatives can no longer rely only on probing questions or discussing product features and benefits. They must do more. They must have access to insights specifically relevant to the target buyer to give them information they didn't know before so as to educate the buyer on the business issues that challenge them. When sales and marketing obtain access to the abundant amount of company data available today, they are able to come to the conversation armed with deeper level insights about the target buyer. This enables them to move from a traditional sales rep trying to determine how their product can somehow fit the buyer to co-creating a solution that provides significant value to the buyer. Increasing the sales rep's knowledge creates immediate value for the buyer and increases the credibility of the sales rep.

An example of how leaders can put this into action is to have marketing monitor the buyer's intent data and share those insights with sales before they connect with buyers. The intent data may show the buyer is considering working with two specific competitors. Armed with this information, the sales rep might focus more time working with the buyer to home in on the solution criteria necessary for their specific business challenge and organizational dynamics. Doing so might help the sales rep rule out one or both the competitors based on the fact that he or she knows that competitor's product is not able to deliver on certain capabilities the buyer needs.

> **TheAlignmentPodcast.com**
> **Episode 10 | Decreasing Time To Revenue Requires**
> **A Focus On Customer Value**
>
> "It's less about selling to the buyer and really about understanding how to communicate with them – how to then help drive forward the sales process along with their journey as opposed to trying to fit them into our traditional sales funnels or stages."
>
> **– Roderick Jefferson,**
> CEO at Roderick Jefferson & Associates, LLC

BUYING HAS BECOME MORE COMPLEX FOR EVERYONE

To understand why selling in B2B has become more complex, leaders have to take a closer look at the changing forces impacting today's buyer. By examining information from their perspective, leaders can begin to see how they can uniquely position the company as a customer-focused organization that has a primary goal of creating value for its customers.

Some of the key factors that have made buying more complex for B2B buyers are:

- Buying teams are increasing in size and may now consist upwards of 10 key stakeholders.[17]

- Most buying decisions are now made by consensus rather than one executive who acts as the company's purchasing agent.

- Buyers are more socially connected to peer groups and thus more influenced by their opinions and decisions.

- Millennials are joining buying groups and tend to be skeptical of claims made by sellers, especially if they are not backed by credible data/research.

- The cost of choosing the wrong vendor is higher (e.g. poor adoption by the organization, career reputation, negative impact on company morale).

- There are often several available solutions on the market, causing the buying group to be overwhelmed and unable to reach a consensus.

- Buyers are expected to conduct a significant amount of research on their own using a multitude of online and offline channels.

What this means for B2B sellers is:

- They must ensure they are aware of all key stakeholders and influencers involved in the company's decision-making process and provide personalized experiences that take these factors into account.

- Content must provide value at every step in the buyer's journey and resonate with the specific persona for which it was created.

- They must be able to clearly communicate the expected outcome(s) if the buyer chooses to work with their company.

---

17   Wixom, Spencer. 2018, November. "More B2B Decision Makers Are Weighing In." Retrieved from https://www.challengerinc.com/blog/more-b2b-decision-makers-want-in

- They must be flexible in the selling process and ready to provide buyers the information they desire, regardless whether it comes from sales or marketing.

- They must focus on executing an excellent customer experience (CX) that makes the buying process as seamless and frictionless as possible.

THE NEW BUYER'S JOURNEY IS NON-LINEAR

With this increased access to information and consensus-based decision making, the buyer's journey looks nothing like the traditional linear, step-wise process that has been the industry standard for a long time. What today's B2B companies have to recognize is that no matter what their product or service, they are selling change. And change is not a linear process, especially when dealing with human beings.

The new sales process is fluid and accompanies buyers as they go back and forth between stages, attempting to validate what they've learned and create consensus within the buying team. Thus, sellers must adopt a process that is agile and can respond to the ever-changing needs of the buyer. Instead of only being focused on available resources in the sales or marketing silos, leaders must be aware of all cross-functional resources available to effectively orchestrate the best experience for each target buyer. Today's buyers see sales and marketing teams as one. So should company leaders.

BUYER'S WANT HELP EARLY IN THEIR JOURNEY

It is true that buyers are conducting more independent research and connecting with sellers much later in the buying journey. Many companies consider this to be a difficult challenge to overcome, and they have reacted by aggressively sending buyers more sales pitches during the final stages of the journey. This approach causes sellers to bombard target buyers through every channel known (e.g. email, social, cold calling, webinars, etc.) to gain their attention. With companies using the same aggressive outreach tactics, buyers have become immune to outreach from companies they don't know. How many times have you answered the phone from a number you didn't recognize? Probably very rarely. So why would a buyer in the final stages of their buying journey want to engage with an unknown company trying to sell them something? Sellers must develop a relationship early on in the buyer's journey, and they can do so by providing value right from the beginning.

TheAlignmentPodcast.com
Episode 03 | Higher-Value Conversations Lead To More Deals

"I don't see much conversation from either side right now about what we need to do to be able to serve the client where we find them. Mostly it's about us. It's either more about us on the sales side in that we want to jam them into this process that we have. ...or it's from the marketing side and we say this is what we think about where the buyer is, and we don't really do a very good job of aligning those two things."

– Anthony Iannarino,
keynote speaker and bestselling author of *Eat Their Lunch*

BUYERS WANT A VALUE-FIRST RELATIONSHIP

For buyers, value in the early stages of the journey comes in the form of content and interactions that educate them on the business challenges they face. This content must be focused on empowering the buyer with a new understanding of whatever issue they need to solve. To support the sales team, marketing must ensure this type of content is readily available in all the major channels that target buyers trust and use to educate themselves. Sales doesn't have the time or reach to educate as many target buyers as marketing can, and that's why it's crucial that sales leaders leverage marketing's ability to effectively reach larger numbers of potential customers.

If sales leaders don't engage with their marketing counterpart, they will not be able to ensure the most effective messages are shared with the marketplace. It is the sales leader's responsibility to do everything in their power to enable sales reps to initiate conversations with the right types of buyers.

Marketers must keep in mind that today's buyers are not spending much time on the company's branded website in the beginning of their journey. During this period, they want as much objective information as possible and assume information on the company page will be geared toward selling. Thus, not only should marketing have content focused on educating buyers on the company website, this information must also be present in channels like third-party review sites, industry publications, blogs, and more. As buyers find myriad educational resources, they validate the information learned.

Sales should partner with marketing to leverage the same type of educational content to position themselves as subject matter experts in their outreach, in-person and on social media. This is referred to as social selling. When target buyers see sales professionals can discuss more than just their product's features and benefits, they are seen more as trusted advisors instead of traditional sales reps pushing a product. These combined efforts aimed at educating target buyers will provide significant value and help build a relationship of trust between the buyer and seller.

TheAlignmentPodcast.com
Episode 29 | Influencers Significantly Impact
The Sales Process

"There are more people engaged in the sales process as influencers than ever before. So, buyers are spending less time in front of salespeople and dramatically more time in front of other people virtually or in person – researching, gaining knowledge, educating themselves, and getting referrals."

— Colleen Francis,
Hall of Fame keynote speaker and
award-winning sales strategist

THE POWER OF INFLUENCERS

Influencers also play a larger role in the decisions modern buyers make.[18] Influencers include connections such as professionals, peers, analysts, and industry thought-leaders. As buyers have become more socially connected, these influencers play a larger role in how buyers make decisions. Buyers often reach out to peers in the network for vendor recommendations, read top analyst reports, and look to industry thought-leaders for their opinions on trends or even specific vendors. Both sales and marketing leaders must ensure they are focused on conversations with key stakeholders within the target account's buying team and are also engaged with external influencers that have significant impact on how buyer's buy.

BUYERS WANT A STRATEGIC BUSINESS PARTNER

The modern buyer now demands a different type of buyer-seller relationship. Most B2B purchases are a complex process that spans several months to a year, so buyers don't want vendors who are solely focused on a simple, one-time transactional sell. They want to work with vendors that can help them analyze and solve complex challenges they face now and in the future. They want vendors focused on building long-term relationships by providing significant value from the start. They want to work with strategic business advisors who perform as if they are already a part of the internal decision-making team. This is the type of seller the modern buyer will reward with a closed deal and repeat business.

---

18   Brito, Michael. 2018, May. "The Year of Influencer Marketing for B2B Brands." Retrieved from https://marketingland.com/2018-the-year-of-influencer-marketing-for-b2b-brands-240357

Strategic business advisors tend to have a number of distinct traits that leaders must encourage in their team and company culture[19]. They must:

- Be highly focused on buyer's needs, rather than on their own goals or objectives.

- Help the buyer clearly define their goals and ensuring that actions they take are aligned with those goals.

- Look at how the decisions made today will impact the buyer's business in the future.

- Have domain expertise and the ability to share relevant insights.

- Believe that if they help the buyer solve problems, they will reward them with their business.

- Focus on earning buyer's trust from the beginning of the relationship by providing upfront and tangible value.

- Actively listen much more than they speak.

Leaders must move away from the traditional transactional selling style of the past and accept that buyers want to build relationships with vendors based on trust and value. When leaders can position their companies as forward-thinking organizations that want to co-create solutions with buyers, they will win with modern buyers.

---

19   Maister, D., Green, C., & Galford, R. 2001. *The Trusted Advisor*. New York: Touchstone.

CHAPTER 6

A Three Pillar Framework for Alignment Transformation

"Remarkable visions and genuine insights are always met with resistance. And when you start to make progress, your efforts are met with even more resistance. . . . The yin and yang are clear: without people pushing against your quest to do something worth talking about, it's unlikely to be worth the journey. Persist."

— Seth Godin,
Tribes: We Need You to Lead Us

Before an alignment transformation can begin, there must be buy-in from senior leadership, including the CEO.[20] Aligning sales and marketing is not just a functional or departmental issue, it's an organizational issue. Alignment is about business transformation and increasing cross-functional collaboration with arguably the most important part of the company – the one responsible for generating revenue. If senior leadership and the CEO are not on board with this effort, it will not work. That's why it's crucial to be able to articulate the true cost of misalignment and be able to demonstrate the business case for why allocating resources to an initiative like this is worth the effort.

The Harvard Business Review article, "How Aligned is Your Organization," points to four main reasons why misalignment in organizations exists:

---

20   Eiler, Tracy & Austin, Andrea. 2016. *Aligned to Achieve: How to Unite Your Sales and Marketing Teams into a Single Force for Growth*. Hoboken, N.J.: John Wiley & Sons

- **Leaders are unaware of the risk of misalignment**
  The CEO and senior leadership must start to look at sales and marketing as a revenue-generation system (a Revenue Engine) and understand the risks associated with inaction when it comes to aligning their efforts. Leaders can no longer put their heads in the sand about the misalignment present between these two very important revenue-generating functions. If a company has any plans to achieve significant growth, misalignment must be at the top of the list of strategic priorities.

- **Nobody "owns" alignment**
  The CEO must be the key sponsor of any alignment effort. As this is a business transformation effort, it is imperative that the CEO be the voice and face to let rank-and-file employees know that the organization has committed to making alignment a priority. Without his/her support, there will be too many middle managers fighting to protect their fiefdoms instead of thinking about the overall health of the organization.

- **Complexity makes alignment that much harder**
  Achieving growth in B2B has become more difficult. We must set realistic expectations; the work associated with aligning these teams will not happen overnight. The dysfunctional relationship between sales and marketing has persisted for decades. We not only need to transform processes in place, we need to transform the way salespeople and marketers understand their relationship with each other. When we can create greater empathy between these two teams and help them understand how much they need each other to achieve success, it becomes easier to get people to take action with the right motivation and intention.

- **Activity is mistaken for progress**
  Setting a clear vision, definitive goals, and measurable objectives upfront is an absolute must. Success metrics used must have a direct impact on revenue. Otherwise, we focus on metrics that make us feel good about our activity but don't necessarily move the business forward. This may be a departure for many who have been able to hide behind vanity metrics, but we must all become a bit more transparent to make the organization as competitive as possible.

GETTING READY FOR TRANSFORMATION

Achieving alignment requires change. Change of any kind is typically not easy for most. We instinctively don't like change. If leaders want to successfully align sales and marketing in the organization, and be sure of its sustainability, they must first ensure that all involved in the transformation are onboard for the desired change. Any leaders who are not fully onboard risk keeping the company from building a high-performance Revenue Engine. A fear of change or a denial of the advantages of alignment can influence others in the management hierarchy. Thus, it is imperative to evaluate where the leadership team and management stand in their desire to commit to a transformation of this magnitude. If the time is not taken to do this type of work, aligning sales and marketing will be a short-lived effort.

If leaders are resistant to alignment transformation, it's important to understand why. Many times, it is because they are uniformed or underinformed on the significant benefits of aligning sales and marketing to accelerate revenue growth. Leaders also may underestimate the negative consequences of inaction. It's important to change these opinions on alignment, and that can be done by ensuring they understand the evidence both intellectually and emotionally. Beyond facts and figures, it's key for leaders to see how much easier closing new deals would be if sales and marketing operated as a seamless revenue-generating system.

Leaders should hold meetings devoted to understanding how alignment transformation will impact the business. In these meetings leaders would benefit by discussing topics such as the pros and cons of taking on this type of transformation, the long-term costs of inaction, identifying existing gaps in skill sets, and how conducive the current culture is to successfully accomplishing this type of change. Working with an outside consultant will help the team gain an objective viewpoint of how these two teams currently work together. Generally, getting an unbiased and accurate assessment of the sales-marketing relationship is difficult from an inside perspective. An outsider's objective perspective will allow leaders to benchmark against other companies and current industry trends. This will help leaders understand where the organization is and where it needs to go.

Once leaders agree on the benefits of an alignment transformation and are open to change, it's important to develop a roadmap showing how the organization will move forward. This preparation should include creating a clear picture of how the organization will operate differently after the transformation. To achieve this, leaders should connect with outside peers who have achieved a similar transformation in their organizations, attend conferences or mastermind groups to help gain awareness of the milestones that need to be accomplished, and create an action plan that clearly identifies the work that needs to be done. It is also critical to identify the small steps that need to be taken to achieve the desired milestones. Implementing these will help leaders and the organization gain confidence that alignment is possible. These small projects will also help the organization learn, so when it advances to larger projects, they can be effectively executed with little to no disruption to the business.

During this period of change, it is not about perfection, but progress. Sales and marketing are learning a new way to coexist. Like any major change in business or life, it takes time and repetition to get it right. To provide the organization the best chance of successfully navigating this upcoming alignment transformation, leaders must ensure they develop certain organizational elements to make change easier for everyone. These elements work together to create an environment that enables change and minimizes resistance from either team.

6 Key Imperatives for Transformation[21]

- **Sense of Urgency**: For a change process to be successful, management and employees must understand why transformation is necessary and must feel its urgency. This may entail creating incentives that tie the desired new behaviors to compensation. One incentive to consider is tying marketing's variable compensation directly to a revenue goal. This will ensure that the marketing team is acting in the best interest of their sales colleagues and focusing on activities to increase their ability to close more business.

- **Clear and Shared Vision**: Successful change relies heavily on teams understanding what's in it for them (e.g. increased sales, higher-quality leads, and increased bonus payouts). Not only should the vision articulate how the organization will look in the future, it also should focus on how sales and marketing will do it together.

- **CEO Sponsorship**: For an alignment effort to become part of the company's way of doing business, the CEO must champion the work needed to ensure everyone understands and accepts this is the new direction. The CEO's involvement must go beyond support; it must be woven into all of his/her communication with the organization.

- **Culture of Transparency**: It's been said that culture eats strategy for breakfast. In implementing an alignment transformation, this couldn't be truer. The CEO must support transparency at all levels of the organization. Senior leaders must create an environment where middle management feels safe to discuss what is and is not working without the fear of repercussions.

---

21   Ashkenas, Ron. 2015, January. "We Still Don't Know the Difference Between Change and Transformation." Retrieved from https://hbr.org/2015/01/we-still-dont-know-the-difference-between-change-and-transformation

- **Clearly Defined Milestones**: People like roadmaps to know where they are going. So it is with a company's plans for the future. All leaders must communicate expectations and be open to discussion regarding such.

- **Recognition of Cross-Functional Wins**: Leaders should share stories of how increased collaboration between sales and marketing has led to improved outcomes for the Revenue Engine. Shared outcomes can be reduced sales cycles, increased conversion rates on key cross-functional metrics, or the winning of a new large account.

With these elements in place and the CEO on board as the key sponsor, the sales and marketing leaders can join forces and focus on bridging the gap between these two functions. As salespeople and marketers are shown a new way, it is crucial to focus on the pain everyone shares – connecting with the modern buyer and winning their business. When companies continue to focus on the primary needs of the Revenue Engine rather than the individual function, it begins to change the way members of both teams view their relationship with each other. This new partnership enables the company to satisfy the new and complex demands of the modern buyer. Equal involvement from both teams is absolutely necessary to provide the customer experience that will separate the organization from its peers. Hence why leaders must learn to — create togetherness.

THE THREE PILLARS OF ALIGNMENT TRANSFORMATION

So how do leaders turn this vision of alignment into a reality?

Many things need to happen to accomplish this. Leaders must understand that, in order to execute this type of transformation successfully, it takes time, commitment, vision, and leadership. And they can be assured that the benefits will be far greater than imagined and the transformation will be a competitive game-changer for any B2B business.

Through my work with clients, speaking and conferences, and hosting *TheAlignmentPodcast.com*, three themes emerged as the backbone of turning an alignment transformation into a reality. The Three Pillars of Alignment Transformation are Data, Process, and Communication. For leaders to achieve successful alignment between sales and marketing, strategic changes must take place in each of these areas. One missing element will result in an unsuccessful or short-lived transformation effort. For sustainable revenue growth to occur, these three pillars provide a valuable framework for structuring the work necessary to build a high-performing Revenue Engine where sales and marketing act as one team.

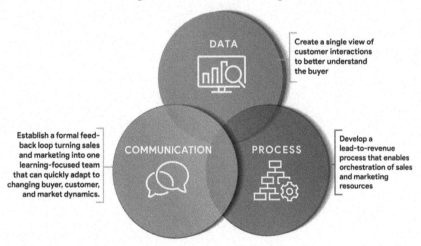

Create a Lasting Transformation Using the 3 Pillars of Alignment

DATA

Create a single view of customer interactions to better understand the buyer

Establish a formal feedback loop turning sales and marketing into one learning-focused team that can quickly adapt to changing buyer, customer, and market dynamics.

COMMUNICATION

PROCESS

Develop a lead-to-revenue process that enables orchestration of sales and marketing resources

Figure 3: The 3 Pillars of Alignment Transformation Framework

If a company focuses on data and process without communication, they will not be able to learn and adapt as buyers' needs change. If process and communication are changed without focusing on data, learning about the buyer will be a guessing game. If communication and data are the only focus without a formal process in place, the company will not have the structure to know what is and is not delivering desired outcomes. Thus, it is absolutely necessary to address all three pillars to ensure this effort is successful.

CHAPTER 7

Pillar 1: Data

Objective: *Create a single view of customer interactions to better understand the buyer*

Data is the currency of the modern B2B business. Many estimate that it is now even more valuable than oil. The advances in sales and marketing technology allow greater access to this massive increase in data. Every phone call, email, downloaded white paper, "like" of a post, and more are all additional data points that provide deeper insight into customer and buyer behavior and preferences. Though rich data can show how to approach and interact with target buyers, most companies are not leveraging that available information. Many companies that do take an active role in monitoring their data do so without the ability to interpret what is there because the data sits in separate silos throughout the organization.

DATA IS ALIVE

The health of company data must be maintained. In today's rapidly changing business environment, B2B customer data has an average shelf life of about three years.[22] Old data is like operating a sports car with dirty oil. The engine becomes less efficient, runs hotter than it should, and ultimately losses horsepower. The same can be said about the Revenue Engine. Sales and marketing teams become less efficient at closing deals, they overwork themselves to compensate for focusing on the wrong types of accounts, and the company's ability to achieve its growth goals is severely compromised.

22   Davis, J. (Producer). 2019, July 25. "How to Make Better Decisions Using the Right B2B Data," with Dave Elkington [Audio podcast]. Retrieved from https://www.jeff-davis2.com/thealignmentpodcast-raw/2019/7/25/ep-37-not-all-b2b-data-is-created-equal-w-dave-elkington

"Too many organizations lack synergy in their sales and marketing efforts because they don't have the data they need to set goals, measure results, and refine their approach. This starts with having one view of the customer but ends with having one view of the results of your strategy."

– Antwoine Flowers, Ph.D
data scientist at Google

CREATE A SINGLE SOURCE OF TRUTH

Sales and marketing leaders struggle to achieve their revenue goal when they have only half the picture. It's like trying to operate a complex system with one eye closed. You lose many of the finer details as well as your depth perception, surrendering the ability to put things into context. With the B2B buying process becoming more complex and demanding, how can leaders develop strategies with only half the story?

First, sales and marketing leaders need to create a single source of truth. This will result in:

- Reduced conflict for the revenue team.
- Marketing being able to demonstrate ROI for its activities, as well as its contribution to pipeline.
- Dashboards that display the entire revenue-generation process to better manage opportunities, improved forecasting accuracy, and identify problem areas in the buying process.

Creating this single source of truth requires more than unifying and cleansing the data. It makes sense of all the available data sources so the company is able to develop insights about its customers and target buyers. Unifying the data can be complex, as it requires establishing a stable identifier across different data sources.[23] Companies may have several different tools that use unique identifiers for customer interactions, but without a stable identifier, data

---

23   Fry, Ed. 2018, October. "How To Create A Single Source Of Truth For Your Customer Data." Retrieved from https://www.hull.io/blog/single-source-of-truth/

cannot be sorted and matched. Having a strong sales and marketing operations team can help alleviate this challenge.

Some high-level steps to think about as the company begins the journey to creating a single view of the customer are:

- Connecting all sources of customer data (i.e. email, CRM, web leads, etc.).

- Determining how to create unique and stable identifiers for buyer and account leads.

- Cleansing and standardizing data to ensure it is reliable.

- Focusing on creating actionable insights for both sales and marketing from the company's customer data.

By investing the time and energy required to create a single view of the customer, leaders will enable sales and marketing to work together, create more personalized customer experiences, and develop a more efficient revenue generation process.

Although there is much to do, a good way to start is by having joint sales and marketing meetings, or by renaming them revenue team meetings where both functions discuss what they are seeing in their data. Things will not be perfect at first (nothing is); however, these meetings will help the team to start focusing on the metrics that are most important and create a more unified vision into how buyers are interacting with the company.

FOCUSING ON METRICS THAT MATTER

Not all data is created equal. As most marketing teams are starting to realize, vanity metrics such as clicks and likes are not directly linked to revenue. Thus, sales and marketing leaders must focus on the metrics that show the highest correlation with converting buyers to customers. The first metric to always focus on is revenue. As calculating marketing ROI becomes more attainable, marketing leaders must take on the responsibility of having a direct impact on building pipeline, just like sales.

Other metrics influenced by both sales and marketing that have a strong impact on revenue growth include:

- End-to-End conversion rates
- Sales cycle length
- Average deal size
- MQL(marketing qualified lead)-to-opportunity ratio

By focusing on the metrics that have the most impact on closing business, leaders can ensure team incentives are aligned and that everyone is laser focused on doing the things that have the most impact on improving business outcomes.

ALIGN GOALS

In addition to focusing on cross-functional metrics that have a direct impact on achieving business objectives, leaders must also ensure sales and marketing have aligned goals. The goals set for sales and marketing cannot be constructed in a vacuum. They must be created from an understanding of the entire revenue-generation process. By starting with the desired revenue goal and backing into what needs to happen for the teams to achieve that goal, teams can set goals that are realistic and directly related to one another. Thus, if teams determine a certain number of MQLs are needed to hit a revenue target, marketing understands that the number is not arbitrary and will negatively impact sales if it's not hit. Sales will either miss the revenue target or be forced to adjust other metrics to compensate. Creating goals in this way reinforces the concept that everyone's actions are interrelated and critical to achieving the ultimate goal of hitting the revenue target.

DISCOVER THE IDEAL CUSTOMER

Sales and marketing teams often don't have a clear understanding or agreement on who is the ideal customer. I've worked with organizations where different answers come from the sales and marketing leaders, and sometimes the CEO. This lack of clarity wastes time and energy by going after accounts that have a low or no chance of converting into customers. Many organizations have trouble clearly articulating the type of account that has the best chance of becoming a customer. They continue to operate under the old model of selling to everyone, which is no longer effective for the modern B2B organization. To achieve success in the modern B2B environment, a company must be laser focused on the type of accounts that have the highest likelihood of valuing what the company provides.

Having unified data from which to work allows leaders to have a more complete picture of which account types are converting and where the company should spend their efforts. Ideal customer profiles (ICPs) should be built with combined sales and marketing data. An ICP is first and foremost an economic tool to help focus company resources toward activities that drive revenue growth in the most efficient way possible.

Developing a strong ICP allows leaders to:

- Focus sales and marketing resources on target customers that will provide the highest ROI.

- Develop resources (e.g. messaging, content, collateral, etc.) with the highest probability of engaging and converting target buyers by addressing their unique business challenges, pain points, and triggers.

- Invest in being present in channels that target buyers respect and are considered to be a top resource for educating their teams on potential solutions.

Or, put more simply a good ICP tells us...

- Who is the right customer?

- What's the best message to clearly demonstrate the value the company provides?

- Where are the best places to be so targets will see and hear our message?

The 3 steps to creating a well-developed ICP include the following:

1. Identify your best customers by considering metrics like customer lifetime value (LTV), cost of customer acquisition (CAC), average order value (AOV).

2. Determine what your best customers have in common by considering firmographics, pain points, messaging that resonated with them, etc.

3. Get clarity on the best customers' motivations for buying and internal buying decision-making process by:

   - Interviewing them to get direct feedback.

   - Reviewing customer feedback/complaints directly and at third-party review sites.

   - Asking sales representatives for qualitative feedback on top accounts.

Once leaders have developed the ICP, they must share it with everyone throughout both the marketing and sales teams and clearly articulate how it should be leveraged in the context of each team member's responsibilities.

Simple Ideal Customer Profile Template

COMPANY	CUSTOMER 1	CUSTOMER 2	CUSTOMER 3
FIRMOGRAPHICS			
Industry			
Geography			
Annual Revenue			
# of Employees			
Budget			
Technology/Products for Integration			
BUSINESS FIT			
Key Pain Points			
Business Objectives			
Key Stakeholders			
Purchasing Process			
Internal Champion Role(s)			
MISC INSIGHTS			
Trusted Research Resources			
Key Reason for Buying			

Figure 4: A simple ideal customer profile template

BUYER PERSONAS ALLOW YOU TO BE LASER-FOCUSED

Once an ICP has been established, leaders can move to developing customer personas to help the team get clarity on how they will connect with those who sit within the buying decision-making team at the target company. It is imperative to know who makes up the buying decision team because the groups are constantly growing, which makes achieving consensus ever more challenging. A majority of deals lost by companies are actually lost to "no deal" because of the inability of sales and marketing to help key stakeholders navigate their internal decision-making process.[24]

Understanding how to do this is extremely challenging, as it is a process that happens behind closed doors. Even if we have a good relationship with buyers on the team, we will never truly understand the complex relationships and processes that come into play to actually arrive at a decision. However, without intimately understanding the stakeholders at the table, we have no chance of ensuring that they get the information that is most relevant to them and addresses

---

24   Bartels, Aaron. 2017, October. "How to Close the Sales Year Strong - and Not Alienate Customers." Retrieved from https://salesbenchmarkindex.com/insights/how-to-close-the-sales-year-strong-and-not-alienate-customers/

their unique priorities. This is where developing action-oriented buyer personas is helpful for both marketers and salespeople.

Developing detailed buyer personas are useful because they force both marketing and sales to think about the key stakeholders involved throughout the buying process. Because this buying group is growing in size, it has become mandatory to take a personalized, multi-faceted approach. The CIO, the Head of Sales, and the CEO have different priorities. A well-crafted buyer persona will help all stay focused on the right stakeholders within the organization and ensure our messaging is not only consistent across both sales and marketing, but has the best chance of actually speaking in a way that meaningfully connects with the target buyer.

These profiles should do more than list title, reporting structure, and personality; they should highlight action-oriented details that can be used to build rapport and help further conversations. The profile should also include information such as resources the buyer trusts, personalized messaging that presents things in their language, what strategic priorities they are focused on, how their performance is evaluated, and trigger events that might put them in an active buying mode. These kinds of details provide valuable insights to help sales and marketing connect with buyers in a meaningfully way. It also allows them to build trust much faster. For example, if ACME Magazine is the most trusted source for a target buyer, marketing should consider submitting content to the publication. Sales could leverage this information in social-selling efforts by sharing the magazine's articles and adding commentary to display intimate knowledge of current industry trends. When a marketing team provides their sales counterparts with deep insights about their target buyers that helps them understand how to create a connection and demonstrate value faster, it builds trust between the two teams.

Sample Customer Persona Profile

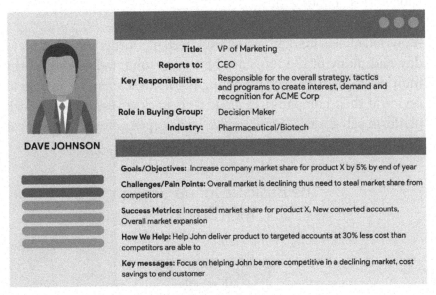

Title:	VP of Marketing
Reports to:	CEO
Key Responsibilities:	Responsible for the overall strategy, tactics and programs to create interest, demand and recognition for ACME Corp
Role in Buying Group:	Decision Maker
Industry:	Pharmaceutical/Biotech

DAVE JOHNSON

Goals/Objectives: Increase company market share for product X by 5% by end of year

Challenges/Pain Points: Overall market is declining thus need to steal market share from competitors

Success Metrics: Increased market share for product X, New converted accounts, Overall market expansion

How We Help: Help John deliver product to targeted accounts at 30% less cost than competitors are able to

Key messages: Focus on helping John be more competitive in a declining market, cost savings to end customer

Figure 5: A simple customer persona profle

DEVELOPING A DATA STACK

This step involves leaders realizing what the true value technology provides is — data. With so much customer interaction data pouring out of these systems, leaders have to be clear about what data points they need and then audit their systems to ensure that the desired data is being captured. This auditing process will lead to better clarity about where gaps exist in the tech stack and where there are redundancies that can be removed.

I'm often asked by companies what sales or marketing tech should be used to ensure they have a high-performing revenue tech stack. This is a misguided question as it supports leaders stacking more and more tech directed at adding additional capabilities. While this might sound like the solution, the result tends to make the sales and marketing process more cumbersome. A more effective approach to optimizing the revenue tech stack is to ensure that the basic tools are covered and that both sales and marketing are leveraging the data these tools provide in the best way. Once that is confirmed, leaders can start to add more complex platforms to increase the capabilities of both teams.

A myriad of new marketing and sales tech platforms come out every day and many of the tools are being consolidated so they cover multiple categories. The following list is for leaders to be able to review if their company's revenue tech stack covers the basic tech platform categories. There are five basic types of tools[25] that must be present to have a complete revenue tech stack.

The Basic Revenue Growth Tech Stack

Figure 6: The 5 basic components of an optimized revenue tech stack

- **Data:** Clean data is the foundation of any stack. Without it, making timely and accurate business decision is difficult.

- **CRM:** When CRM is used properly, this system might be the most valuable tool a company can use to conduct business.

---

25   Davis, J. (Producer). 2018, May. "How to Develop the Best Revenue Tech Stack," with Dan Cilley [Audio podcast]. Retrieved from https://www.jeffdavis2.com/thealign-mentpodcast-raw/2018/5/8/ep-7-

Customer relationships matter most, and a CRM can help track relationships, as well as every touchpoint sales and marketing have had with a buyer. This helps to create an accurate picture of what has transpired throughout the buying journey, while also revealing opportunities that could have been overlooked.

- **Marketing Automation:** Beyond helping to save time and money, it's been proven to increase revenue and ROI. In addition, it allows the marketing team to focus more on an effective strategy rather than ensuring repetitive tasks are completed on time.

- **Onboarding/Training:** Training new sales representatives is costly and time-consuming. It has been repeatedly shown that a high percentage of training content is forgotten within weeks after training. This demonstrates the need for ongoing, dynamic training, which can be achieved with tech-enabled on-boarding tools as needed without the need for a formal training session and time out of the field or not on the phone.

- **Account-based Marketing (ABM):** ABM has proven over time to provide significant ROI because it enables collaboration across the organization to meet the unique goals of the client. In the past, due to cost and complexity, ABM was left to large enterprises to focus on a few highly-valuable accounts. Now with new marketing tech and tools, organizations of all sizes can take advantage of this highly effective strategy to personalize outreach to targeted accounts.

CHAPTER 8

Pillar 2: Process

Objective: *Develop a lead-to-revenue process that enables orchestration of sales and marketing resources*

It's important to build a unified lead-to-revenue process to identify existing challenges in the buyers' journey. Without constructing an end-to-end revenue-generation process, leaders will not be able to pinpoint existing leaks in the revenue funnel. Without a complete picture of buyers' interactions with sales and marketing, the company can't move forward to improve the buying process.

Today's sales funnel is a complex, non-linear process that involves a growing number of stakeholders – all with their own unique priorities. To effectively sell to buyers, companies must stop thinking in terms of sales and marketing funnels, but rather a unified revenue funnel made up of orchestrated interactions between sales, marketing, and target buyers. A revenue funnel focuses on the end-to-end process of acquiring opportunities and converting them into closed business. When leaders are able to assimilate the entire process, they will be able to optimize it, ensure it is aligned with the buyer's internal buying process, and confirm whether the customer experience is one buyers will deem worthy of their budgeted dollars.

The Modern Buyer's Demands

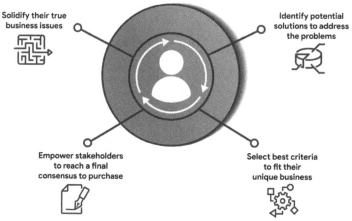

Figure 7: The modern buyer's demands

The revenue-generation process must be flexible and enable sellers to address four key factors for buyers by:

- Helping them solidify their true business issues.
- Identifying potential solutions to address the problems.
- Guiding them to select best criteria to fit their unique business.
- Empowering stakeholders to reach a final consensus to purchase.

Where are most companies getting this process wrong? They:

- Assume the standard linear sales model can still be used with the modern buyer.
- Have a separate sales and marketing funnel with little to no visibility across them.
- Create a process focused on the company's needs and not how buyers buy.
- Focus on which function is responsible for each phase of the process instead of what the buyer needs during each phase of the journey and which function is most adept (sales and/or marketing) at delivering it.

"So there's definitely a switch that happens I think when you start getting more metric driven and start caring about that full funnel. You get way more aligned with sales because their outcomes suddenly become your outcomes."

– Adam Goyette,
VP of Marketing at G2

THE MODERN BUYING CYCLE

Today's buyers will not be coerced into a linear, step-wise sales process. They have been empowered with unlimited access to information and people. In addition, there is no longer one person who signs the check. Companies rely on consensus-driven decision-making; thus companies must engage with a greater number of stakeholders during the revenue-generation process.

Buyer engagement is now more fluid. For example, the buyer may take a discovery call to clarify specific issues that might affect the successful implementation of the product or service, and then engage in additional research to validate information shared by sales. Access to so much information about the product or service has put the buyer in the driver's seat, so leaders must respond with a revenue-generation process that is flexible and allows both marketers and sales representatives to orchestrate the optimal experience to meet buyers wherever they are during the buying cycle.

To identify the optimal resources, both sales and marketing should seek feedback about the internal buying process of their target buyer. This can be done by leveraging the relationships of the company's best customers. Companies should ask customers what they considered in making their purchase so sales and marketing leaders can adapt their approach to selling. Buyers now see salespeople as consultants who are focused on helping them navigate the complex buying cycle. The buying cycle is only representational, but if the seller is willing to seek feedback about the buyers' internal buying process, the seller can develop a map closer to the actual process.

Leaders will recognize that the buying cycle is not about wanting the buyer to do what the selling company wants, but more about helping both sales and marketing better understand the buyer's goals, objectives, and motivation during each stage. By doing so, the team will learn how to engage with the target buyer to deliver a consistent, laser-focused approach. This ensures all sales and marketing colleagues remain customer-focused and that their actions are aligned with the buyer's needs. Changing the company's focus to a buyer's focus will help sales and marketing achieve greater success throughout the revenue-generation process.

Each stage in the buying cycle helps leaders gain clarity on the buyer's needs. Sales and marketing will act as a trusted advisor for buyers to achieve their goals and resolve their business problems.

To orchestrate the best interactions for buyers, leaders must go through the following steps:

- Know the six stages of the modern buying cycle.

- Understand the buyer's motivations during each stage of the cycle.

- Be aware of all seller-buyer interactions so sales and marketing can navigate buyers through the cycle.

STAGE 1: PROBLEM NAIVE

Buyers are unaware they have a major business problem.

Buyer-seller interactions that will resonate: Sellers (sales and marketing) should focus on creating a disruptive, emotional, and compelling message to awaken the buyer to the significant business issues they face. Sellers should also focus on helping buyers identify the symptoms of the issues so they can identify the triggers they should look for.

Resources that can be used:

- Video marketing

- Influencer marketing

- Social media marketing/social selling

STAGE 2: REALIZATION

Once target buyers realize their business faces challenges, they will research all issues to discover the specific business problems they face.

Buyer-seller interactions that will resonate: Sellers should focus on educating buyers to help them understand all the relevant variables so they can narrow the possible causes. Once the problem is discovered, the extent must be quantified so the buyer has the necessary information to discern the depth of the problem. For example, when a roof leaks, can it be patched or must it be replaced entirely? These are similar solutions but on a different scale. Taking a consultative approach over a traditional sales approach creates a relationship built on trust and service. Helping the buyer with all aspects of the problems adds a level of respect that is lacking in the traditional sales approach.

Resources that can be used:

- SEO/SEM

- Social media marketing/social selling

- Podcasts

- Speaking at tradeshows/conferences

- Analyst reports

- eBooks

STAGE 3: EXPLORATION

With a clear understanding of the business problems they face, buyers now look to explore all the potential solutions available.

Buyer-seller interactions that will resonate: Sellers should help buyers understand the different types of solutions that could potentially be used to resolve their business issue. Sellers should help the buyer weigh the pros and cons of each option as well as consider how their choice will impact their long-term company goals.

Resources that can be used:
- Third-party review site listings
- Case studies
- Product webinar
- Sales demo
- Educational field marketing events

STAGE 4: CONFIRMATION

Now that buyers understand which solutions show promise of being a good fit, they look to confirm the specific capabilities required for their unique business challenge and organizational dynamics. These criteria will help them develop a short list of vendors and ultimately be able to choose the right one for the company.

Buyer-seller interactions that will resonate: Sellers should focus on demonstrating to the buyer that they understand what solution capabilities are important to them. Sellers can also share how other companies with similar profiles have been able to leverage their solution successfully. If it is clear what capabilities are most important to the buyer, sellers may want to provide a direct comparison to competitors that shows how their solution is a better match.

Resources that can be used:
- Competitor comparison charts
- Solution impact calculators
- Personalized sales videos
- Consultative sales call

STAGE 5: DECISION

Target buyers are clear which solutions can meet their needs and make a final decision on which company they think will be the best fit. Many factors beyond solution capabilities come into play, such as the overall buying experience and how they envision working with the company.

Buyer-seller interactions that will resonate: Seller should focus on demonstrating how intimately they understand the company's goals and will act as a trusted advisor and partner to help them achieve those goals. Interactions should be highly personalized and feel as if they have already started working with the seller.

Resources that can be used:
- Free trial
- Customer success stories
- Testimonials
- Personalized implementation plan

STAGE 6: EVALUATION

Once the buyer becomes a customer, they are continually evaluating whether they made the right decision, are achieving the results they expected, and want to continue working with the vendor. This cycle will begin again when the seller helps the buyer uncover another problem they can help solve or the buyer wishes to expand its use of the company's products or services.

Buyer-seller interactions that will resonate: Seller should focus on reinforcing the reasons why the buyer chose to work with the company. These interactions should continue to build trust and demonstrate the seller's commitment to ensuring success. The buyer should feel like they've added a strategic partner to the team to help them achieve their company goals.

Resources that can be used:

- Customer success services

- Scheduled follow-ups from sales to ensure progress

- Content that shows major milestones that the customer should be accomplishing

- Comparison benchmarks

CONSIDER AN ACCOUNT-BASED STRATEGY

The Pareto Principle reminds us that 20 percent of our efforts lead to 80 percent of our results. Yet, many B2B companies lack focus on targeting the best types of accounts. One way to achieve better focus and encourage increased alignment between sales and marketing is to consider implementing an account-based strategy, also known as account-based marketing (ABM). Account-based strategy more accurately describes the process, as it considers sales as an integral part of the process. Account-based strategy begins with sales and marketing working together to identify the best target accounts, using both quantitative and qualitative inputs. To more clearly define an account-based strategy, it "...is the coordination of highly valuable personalized experiences across all functions that impact the customer and the goal is to drive engagement and conversion at a targeted set of accounts." says Craig Rosenberg, Co-founder and Chief Analyst at TOPO, Inc. (*TheAlignmentPodcast.com*, Episode 38).

Many companies have implemented an account-based strategy with little to no input from sales on which target accounts should be included in campaigns. This is a significant miss and detrimental to the success of implementing this type of strategy. Sales has highly valuable qualitative information about the stakeholders within an account that can affect whether an account should be on the target list. For instance, if a key stakeholder has a strong personal relationship with a competitor and refuses to do business with the company, it may not be worth going after this account. Although the metrics and the revenue potential might make the account a fit, this type of account insight is critical in letting leadership know the likelihood of the team being able to convert the account to a customer.

Account-based strategy has also been shown to be highly effective in driving revenue growth. Here are some of the benefits of implementing this type of strategy:[26]

- **Increased Revenue Generation Efficiency**: By orchestrating the efforts of sales and marketing on a small number of high-value accounts, companies can avoid wasting time, budget, and efforts.

- **Larger Deal Sizes**: Limiting sales efforts to large, high-value accounts means the company wins big when the efforts are successful.

- **Higher Close Rates**: Because the approach is aligned, disciplined, and systematic, and sales and marketing execute it concurrently, it performs much better than the standard linear or ad-hoc approach.

- **Sales Acceleration**: Using a surround-sound approach that delivers personalized content to all the key stakeholders helps the buying teams of target accounts reach consensus much faster.

- **Increased Sales and Marketing Alignment**: By its definition, an account-based strategy requires sales and marketing to co-create a go-to-market strategy.

---

26   Engagio. 2019. *The Clear & Complete Guide to Account Based Marketing - Second Edition.* Retrieved from https://info.engagio.com/rs/356-AXE-401/images/engagios-abm-guide-2nd-edition.pdf

An account-based strategy can be implemented by an organization of any size. To determine if this type of strategy is the best fit for the company, leaders must consider the shape of the company's target market. If the company sells to a highly-targeted market where multiple stakeholders influence the buying decision, then the organization can likely benefit from leveraging an account-based strategy. Many B2B companies fall into the category of being able to benefit from an account-based strategy, but to be successful, they must have enough of the right type of accounts to make the effort worthwhile.

Leaders should consider these additional criteria when making a decision to pursue an account-based strategy:

- A well-defined ideal customer profile (ICP) that's led to closed deals.

- Average sales cycle should be several months, not days.

- Several key stakeholders exist in the target account's buying decision group.

- Marketing has the bandwidth to produce personalized content for target accounts or the budget to hire an outside agency for support.

- Leadership is on board and available for events and experiences created for targeted accounts

TheAlignmentPodcast.com
Episode 38 | 5 Elements of A Bulletproof
Account-Based Strategy

"Account based is the epitome of creating togetherness."

– Craig Rosenberg,
Co-founder and Chief Analyst at TOPO, Inc.

KEY STEPS TO AN ACCOUNT-BASED STRATEGY

Developing an account-based strategy can seem overwhelming if leaders haven't executed a highly complex and orchestrated effort between sales and marketing in the past. Below is a high-level roadmap to help the team understand the steps necessary to implementing this type of strategy.[27]

1. **Discover and Define High-value Accounts:** Use all available data (internal and external) to determine which accounts have high value potential and are worth the time to pursue in this way. Be sure to look beyond firmographic information and include qualitative input from sales to develop a more robust account-selection criteria.

2. **Identify Key Stakeholders and Map Out How Decisions Are Made:** Map the internal structure of each account to understand who the key stakeholders are, as well as the influencers. Be sure to also develop a stakeholder map so everyone is clear on the role each stakeholder plays. This will ensure the entire team is clear about the intent of the communication being shared with the stakeholder.

3. **Map Out Content Along With Personalized Messaging:** Audit current company content and be certain it delivers value in helping the target account understand their business challenges and correlates with the different phases of the buyer's journey. If gaps are found in available content, marketing should develop the needed material. Also, ensure that each piece of collateral is developed with personalized messaging to the individual stakeholder. For example, don't use the same sales piece for the tech lead and the head of marketing.

4. **Determine Optimal Channels:** Consider which channel (e.g. social, email, events, direct mail, etc.) will be the most effective for each stakeholder. Take into account the targeted industry and how each stakeholder's day-to-day schedule is organized. For example, if a target is not behind a desk for the majority of the day, email may not be the optimal channel to communicate with them.

---

27   Marketo. 2019. "What is Account-Based Marketing?" Retrieved from https://www. marketo.com/account-based-marketing/

5. **Execute Targeted and Coordinated Campaigns:** Create a coordinated plan or calendar between sales and marketing so that everyone is clear on what the scheduled touches are for each account and corresponding stakeholders. This document should be easily accessible so everyone is aware of what the target account is receiving. If this process becomes too complex for the team, leaders may consider implementing ABM tech to specifically address this challenge.

6. **Track Results and Adjust:** Be sure to continually monitor each campaign's performance and share results with sales and marketing. Doing this ensures that either team can quickly make adjustments, if necessary, and also allows flexibility if an account needs to be taken out of the established communication sequence. Metrics should be agreed upon before launching an account-based strategy so that everyone is clear about what good looks like. Key metrics to evaluate account-based strategy success include: target account pipeline, account engagement rate, reach, and closed-won target accounts.

MEASURING ALIGNMENT EFFICIENCY

Alignment is more than just having more meetings or getting along better. We must be able to measure alignment to ensure the steps taken are having a positive effect on increasing revenue in the most efficient way. Leaders can miss the mark by only focusing on top and bottom of the funnel metrics and will not understand what to do to optimize the entire revenue-generation process. With this lack of visibility into the inner workings of the system, leaders are constricted to pulling only two levers to increase revenue:

- Push more leads into the system, which leads to focusing purely on volume and may degrade the quality of the leads being shared with sales.

- Push harder to squeeze more out of what sales is receiving from marketing, which can lead to salespeople wasting time by chasing leads with little to no chance of conversion.

Ignoring how buyers respond to interactions cripples the ability of both sales and marketing leaders to adjust their approach to better respond to buyers' needs. When sales and marketing leaders can visualize across the entire buyer's journey, they are able to gain insights such as:

- What marketing content leads to the highest close rates.

- What stage of the buyer's journey experiences the highest drop-off rate.

- Top revenue-producing channels.

- Average lead-to-revenue cycle time.

Insights such as these allow both sales and marketing leaders to optimize the revenue-generation process and focus on growth efficiency instead of hoping for a marginal increase in output, if any at all. The danger in only increasing sales activity or marketing spend, especially if done in a silo, is that certain costs associated with generating revenue may go overlooked (e.g. marketing spend, waste of salespeople's time, additional sales headcount, etc.) If not evaluated in a holistic way, those overlooked costs could outpace revenue gains and actually result in a net loss for the company. However, leaders will never know this if they are not actively tracking and evaluating the growth efficiency of the Revenue Engine.

Leaders should use a number of key metrics to evaluate the growth efficiency of the Revenue Engine. Here are some they can track on their revenue funnel dashboard:

- **Revenue Goal Attainment**: Percentage of annual revenue goal achieved.

- **Customer Acquisition Cost (CCA)**: Total sales and marketing resources associated with acquiring a new customer.

- **Customer Lifetime Value (CLV)**: Average revenue or profit a customer will generate before they churn.

- **Cost of Net New ARR (for SaaS companies)**: Cost to acquire one net new dollar of ARR or total sales and marketing spend divided by net new ARR bookings.

- **Conversion Rates**: Percentage of leads that progress to the next phase in the revenue generation process.

- **Lead to Revenue Conversion Rate**: Percentage of incoming leads that convert to closed deals.

It's important to focus on full revenue funnel metrics as the alignment process continues so sales and marketing can see how efficient the revenue funnel is becoming. If leaders only look at siloed metrics, they may be missing key indicators showing that things are not working as planned. For instance, if the company wins several new large accounts and leaders only look at siloed sales metrics, it may appear that all the work sales and marketing did to close these big accounts was successful. However, if we take a broader system approach in evaluating revenue generation efficiency, we may find the cost of acquiring those new customers was extremely high, maybe even higher than the amount of revenue they generated for the company. It's key to ensure that, as sales and marketing start working closer together, leaders look at full revenue funnel metrics first. Then dig deeper into the functional metrics to be able to paint a clear picture of what is really happening inside the revenue funnel.

CHAPTER 9

Pillar 3: Communication

Objective - *Establish a formal feedback loop turning sales and marketing into one learning-focused team that can quickly adapt to changing buyer, customer, and market dynamics.*

Effective communication is vital to successfully aligning teams. It results from more than just having additional meetings. Effective communication happens when the intended message is successfully delivered, received, and understood. In addition, this communication must be formalized and focused to achieve a specific outcome. How many times have leaders and management met over and over again on the same issue, and nothing gets resolved?

ESTABLISH A CLEAR VISION

A company vision is paramount to creating the glue that will keep sales and marketing aligned for the long term. Communicating a vision creates a beacon far into the future that both teams can look to when times become difficult in the transformation process. Without this "North Star," teams can become weighed down by day-to-day operations and may regress to placing collaboration low on their list of priorities. The start of an alignment transformation is an opportunity to refresh the reason the company exists and what the entire team is trying to achieve. It's also a great opportunity to switch to a customer-focused approach from a product-focused approach if the company hasn't done so already.

TheAlignmentPodcast.com
**Episode 36 | Changing The Dysfunctional Sales
and Marketing Narrative**

"A leader's job is to make sure everybody feels ownership of the results they've asked them to achieve. Everybody must be fully enlisted into the aspiration you're trying to achieve. That means you've taken the time to help them understand what that aspiration is, and how they fit into it. Just "announcing it" is useless. If all people understand is *what* you want, then you have compliance. Mere adherence to the plan. But, if they understand how what you want fits into *their* purpose, how they *want to* contribute, then you have passion and commitment on top of adherence. That's the discretionary effort you need to actually achieve excellent results."

— **Ron Carucci,**
bestselling author of *Rising to Power: The Journey of Exceptional Executives*, and Managing Partner at Navalent

A well-crafted vision paints a clear picture of what the organization wants to achieve over the next five to ten years. It should stimulate and motivate sales and marketing professionals about the company's new direction and the vast benefits of making such a pivotal change. The vision must be time-bound and tangible so both sales and marketing can understand and apply what's required to turn the vision into reality.

The CEO must assure staff that all levels of management value and support the vision at all times. Senior leadership should spend a significant amount of time with management to ensure they understand how the vision translates into the work of their individual team members. This reinforcement will help managers articulate how the vision relates to each individual team member's work. During times of significant change within a company, leaders must be able to answer: "Why are we doing this anyway?"

FORMALIZE THE FEEDBACK LOOP

Having informal, ad-hoc meetings is not sufficient in guaranteeing results. Frequent communication is not necessarily effective communication. A formalized feedback loop ensures sales and marketing are in-sync and able to quickly adjust to necessary changes.

Here are a few tactics that can be easily implemented to establish a formal feedback loop and increase effective communication between sales and marketing:

- **Weekly Growth Team Meetings**: Leadership reviews campaign metrics and revenue funnel performance.

- **Quarterly Growth Meetings**: Sales and marketing leaders update the team on revenue performance and highlight successful collaborative wins.

- **Sales Insights**: Leaders develop convenient ways for sales to communicate significant customer insights to the marketing team: dedicated email, chat, surveys, etc.

- **Joint Sales-Marketing Calls** – Marketing leaders accompany sales reps to hear what buyers are saying during the buying process directly.

BUILDING COLLABORATION TAKES TIME AND ACTIVE LEADERSHIP

As leaders embark on the journey to increasing collaboration between sales and marketing, it's important to understand what defines true collaboration. On my podcast, Debra Mashek, Ph.D., Executive Director of Heterodox Academy and Professor of Psychology at Harvey Mudd College, addressed the fluidity of human collaboration, known as the "Collaboration Continuum" and how leaders could leverage psychology to improve the connection between sales and marketing. She stated that "collaboration is not a one-time event nor is it an on/off switch. Collaboration happens over a spectrum and takes time, trust, and effective leadership to have teams achieve a highly collaborative relationship." (*TheAlighnmentPodcast.com*, Episode 04) This model is a substantial asset as it helps leaders understand where the sales-marketing relationship is on the spectrum so they can better understand what capabilities and company support need to be developed to move the team in the right direction.

Collaboration is more than just telling people to get in a room and work it out or have more meetings. It is a series of incremental changes in culture, organizational configuration, and capabilities all focused on creating a cohesive and aligned team.

Collaboration Continuum

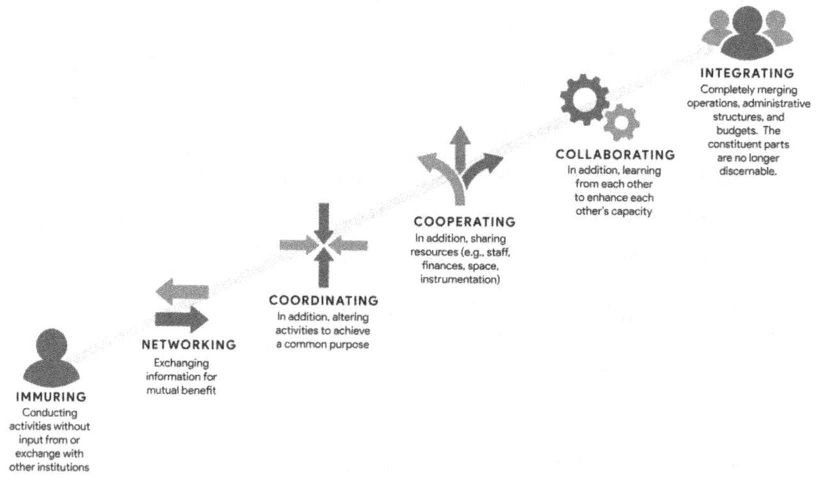

Figure 8: The stages to achieveing true collaboration. Source: Mashek, D. (June, 2015). Capacities and Institutional Supported Needed along the Collaboration Continuum. A presentation to the Academic Deans Committee of The Claremont Colleges, Claremont. CA

THE PATH TO COLLABORATION

The first stage in the Collaboration Continuum model is Immuring. Sales and marketing are considered the two "involved institutions" as referenced in the model. Based on this, the *immuring* stage shows each department conducting activities inside opaque silos as discussed earlier in the book. There is no input from or exchange of information between the two functions. They develop their own plans and execute their work without regard to the other function.

This phase in the continuum correlates extremely well with the "Living Apart Together" stage seen in the sales-marketing configuration model (Malshe and Beiman) discussed in Chapter 4.

The fact that these stages have a lot of the same characteristics is further evidence that leaders should pursue a true alignment transformation when the sales-marketing relationship has reached the "Living Apart Together" configuration stage. When the relationship evolves to a point where sales and marketing are seen as counterparts having similar political standing and influence in the organization, each function will be able to pursue creating togetherness as respected partners.

Moving to the next stage: Leaders can support sales and marketing transitioning into a *networking* relationship by establishing clear communication channels between the two. Opening communication channels will eliminate confusion in delivering information across teams. Leaders should consider investing in tools to help staff more easily connect. These tools could be as simple as a new conference room for larger, more inclusive meetings, video conferencing to help field sales connect to internal meetings, dedicated chat groups to freely exchange ideas and customer insights, and more.

NETWORKING

Networking is the next stage on the continuum. Sales and marketing transition into this stage when they start to exchange information for mutual benefit. Information exchange in this type of relationship tends to be ad-hoc, informal, and unstructured. It may be sales sharing leads received at a trade show, or marketing sharing customer persona profiles they've created with sales. Sales and marketing teams in this stage might share information, but again is it done inconsistently which makes the sharing unreliable and many times less valuable.

Moving to the next stage: Leaders can help sales and marketing transition into a *coordinating* relationship by establishing shared goals and objectives. Leaders can also implement regular performance evaluations to compare stated goals and objectives as well as make necessary adjustments. Implementing an incentive structure more aligned with the achievement of set revenue goals will also encourage the desired changes in increased collaboration.

COORDINATING

The *coordinating* stage represents a willingness from sales and marketing to adjust their activities to support a common goal. An example would be a marketing team that exceeds their quota for MQL volume and receives feedback from sales that conversion rates on leads continue to be low. Through this communication, the marketing leader may find leads are coming from the appropriate types of target accounts but the stakeholders that sales needs to get in front of are underrepresented. The marketing leader could then adjust how they are approaching the market to ensure more of the right stakeholders are presented to the sales team to engage in conversation.

Moving to the next stage: Leaders can help sales and marketing teams transition into the *cooperation* stage by providing guidance on the most effective ways sales and marketing can share resources across teams (e.g. staff, finances, office space. Guidance may include leadership developing processes to help sales and marketing manage a shared budget or headcount.

COOPERATION

In the *cooperation* stage, sales and marketing will do more than just share ideas and feedback. Leaders will share their resources to ensure the Revenue Engine has what it needs to be successful. This could mean activities such as sales and marketing contributing a portion of their budgets to a field event or tradeshow, or the marketing leader working directly with sales representatives on sales calls, or sales helping marketing recruit customers for a customer case study video project, or both teams committing funds for the annual sales kick-off meeting. One innovative arrangement is to have sales and marketing team members complete short-term internships on each other's team. It allows team members to increase their knowledge of the other function and bring an immensely valuable perspective back to their own team.

In this stage, sales and marketing leaders realize that though having their team members work with the other team takes them away from their core responsibilities for a short time, doing so offers positive benefits for all. Having cross-functional interactions and sharing resources helps cross pollenate ideas and keeps the spending on programs in check. As teams share more resources, leaders will want to create guidelines and communicate how resources are to be managed. It's also helpful to choose an objective third party, perhaps the CEO or CFO, to resolve differences that may arise between the sales and marketing leaders.

Moving to the next stage: The most important capacity that leaders need to focus on building when helping their teams transition into a truly collaborative relationship is the opportunity to come together for reciprocal learning.

COLLABORATION STAGE

Collaboration represents the stage where each team actively learns from the other. Learning is a key component indicative of a truly collaborative relationship. Leaders must invest the time and energy to find ways for sales and marketing to come together and learn from each other.

Both sales and marketing make it a priority to act in the best interest of the Revenue Engine over their own personal agenda. In a collaborative environment, sales leaders and representatives alike are compelled to voice concerns with marketing when something is not working. Instead of pointing fingers and blaming marketing for their shortcomings, the sales teams takes an objective approach that is focused on finding better ways of doing things. Sales is also open to modifying their activities to support any necessary changes.

These learning experiences between sales and marketing are delivered both formally and informally in instructor-led and peer-led groups to ensure a variety of viewpoints, information, topics, and communication styles are utilized. The sessions should focus on increasing skill levels of sales representatives and marketers so they can deliver a better CX to target buyers and customers. Here are some good examples of these types of learning experiences:

- Marketing helps sales launch social-selling program and helps them choose top social media channels, relevant resources to find valuable content, and messaging to gain the attention of target buyers.

- Sales shares the internal buying process of a top account; delivering feedback from key stakeholders as well as some major objections experienced during the sales process.

- Conducting a joint win-loss analysis session.

- Marketing sharing industry trends to enhance sales' conversations with target buyers and position them as strategic business partners with their buyers.

- Bringing in speakers to discuss the importance of sales and marketing alignment and how it can help increase effectiveness and efficiency of each team.

INTEGRATING

Transitioning to the *integrating* stage may not be right for every company. This stage may require significant changes to the company's corporate structure, operations, hierarchy, and culture. For a successful transition, leaders will benefit by creating a single point of access to resources and support available to all members of the new organization. This stage is where leaders may decide on new team leadership, revised budget guidelines, and a revised process for decision-making. This process is similar to building a new division at an established corporation. Sales and marketing as the company knew it no longer exists. The two groups now share operations, administrative structure, budgets, programs, planning, culture, and responsibility. This is a true partnership where leaders will blend each function into one new entity.

Reaching the *integrating* stage may prove to be quite difficult and it may not be worth the effort depending on the unique dynamics of the organization. In fact, Malshe and Biemans share that "...the ideal solution is never for a company to merge its sales and marketing departments to create a hybrid entity that understands both the marketing and sales side of the business. Instead, we strongly recommend that sales and marketing maintain their uniqueness and work tirelessly to find common ground, manage their differences, and come together as a team..."

By understanding where sales and marketing are on the Collaboration Continuum, leaders can discern what structure and capabilities need to be put into place to assist both teams transitioning to the next desired stage of their relationship.

CHAPTER 10

Recommendations For Sustaining Togetherness

"You never change things by fighting the existing reality. To change something, build a new model that makes the existing model obsolete."

– Buckminster Fuller

After laying the groundwork for building alignment between sales and marketing, leaders must look to the future to ensure the transformation is sustainable. Below are recommendations on how to continue to strengthen the relationship between sales and marketing. Leading voices in sales, marketing, leadership, and education have shared their insights on how they've helped leaders to stay encouraged and know that great things are coming for the organizations that choose to take the step toward creating togetherness.

9 RECOMMENDATIONS FOR MORE TOGETHERNESS

1. View sales and marketing as one revenue-producing system – a Revenue Engine.
2. Commit to providing the best customer experience possible.
3. Accept the task of becoming comfortable using customer data and insights to better understand the buyer.
4. Tie marketing compensation to pipeline revenue.
5. Consider implementing an account-based strategy.
6. Consolidate the sales and marketing tech stack into a revenue tech stack.

7. Develop a cross-functional enablement council.

8. Leverage AI to increase efficiency and effectiveness.

9. Implement Lead-to-Revenue Tracking (L2R).

1 — VIEW SALES AND MARKETING AS ONE REVENUE-PRODUCING SYSTEM – A REVENUE ENGINE

To create a real change in the DNA of the relationship between sales and marketing, leaders must view and treat the two functions as one revenue-producing system. This new viewpoint must be shared from team leaders all the way up to the CEO. The message must be embedded throughout the organization, so it becomes part of the culture and transforms into "the way we do things."

Leaders should also invest the time to develop more cross-functional experiences. As the lines blur between sales and marketing, the team members will understand how the two functions fit together to produce the best outcomes for the buyer. This togetherness will enable the company to make meaningful connections with target buyers and increase revenue.

———

Iris Chan, CMO at FusionGrove shares her thoughts:

"To be seen as a single revenue engine, both sales and marketing teams must go beyond target buyer personas and take a data-driven, account-focused approach.

Here are some tips to collaboratively drive revenue generation:

- **Step 1**: Jointly define and identify an Ideal Customer Profile (ICP) for each product/service offering in your portfolio.

- **Step 2**: Leverage sales acceleration technologies to surface account-level intelligence and insights about customer organizations — factors that would impact their propensity to adopt your product/service. This helps you to narrow down and target organizations that are the best fit.

- **Step 3**: With a defined set of high-value accounts, you can co-create and orchestrate campaigns for sellers to engage these target customers in guided selling motions, while Marketing executes nurture or outreach activities to create air cover for Sales."

———

Aurélien Gohier, Senior Digital Manager at Dassault Systèmes and Founder of BtoB Marketing & Sales, shares his thoughts on what he calls 360° Workforce Alignment:

"To reach this holy grail, leaders MUST without a doubt make marketers a part of the sales force. This statement is especially true when applied to a complex selling environment. When hired, marketers should spend a few months working hand-in-hand with a salesperson. On-site observations and proper documentation of gained insights are key and should be shared with the internal marketing team.

Sales teams can also benefit from better understanding what B2B marketers do. But the real sales and marketing alignment breakthrough will occur when salespeople and marketers have an equal understanding of what is truly happening in the target market. This is a fundamental step to structuring B2B marketing activities the way they should be. One significant hindrance to achieving sales and marketing alignment is product marketing being handled by the R&D department. This is a mistake which leads to the creation of a gap between sales, marketing, and product development which breaks any hopes of reaching 360° Workforce Alignment. Ultimately, workforce misalignment = lack of a customer-centric business model = low chances of long-term client satisfaction."

———

2 — COMMIT TO PROVIDING THE BEST CUSTOMER EXPERIENCE POSSIBLE

The modern buyer is savvy, informed, and demanding. They will no longer accept difficult-to-navigate buying experiences. Because buyers' loyalty has become a thing of the past, companies must focus on creating a frictionless buying journey. Consider customer interactions with companies such as Netflix, Uber, Amazon, or Zappos. CX has become, in many cases, more important than price or product.

3 — ACCEPT THE TASK OF BECOMING COMFORTABLE USING CUSTOMER DATA AND INSIGHTS TO BETTER UNDERSTAND THE BUYER

Data has become the currency of the B2B business. Companies are sitting on a wealth of customer data, but most are not leveraging it to extract actionable business insights. Data has the power to tell sellers what buyers won't. It has the power to paint a clearer picture of each buyer's needs, wants, desires, preferences, and more. Leaders will not need to become data scientists or experts overnight. They will, however, need to improve their skills in transforming data into usable business insights. With the wealth of data now available through technology, leaders should consider adding a sales and/or marketing operations function to help manage it.

4 — TIE MARKETING COMPENSATION TO PIPELINE REVENUE

If sales and marketing are to act as one team, they must share the same goals and incentives. The most effective incentive driver for many is compensation. When marketing performance metrics and compensation are directly tied to revenue goals, marketing will increase its focus on activities that have the greatest impact on achieving revenue goals. This will also increase the level of respect that sales has for their marketing counterparts leading to an increased willingness to collaborate.

5 — CONSIDER IMPLEMENTING AN ACCOUNT-BASED STRATEGY

Implementing account-based marketing or an account-based strategy has been shown to significantly increase revenue, average deal size, and a number of other important business metrics. This type of strategy aligns sales and marketing from the start and allows both teams to coordinate and execute laser-focused, personalized, and value-driven campaigns. An account-based strategy can be used by any size of organization. Leaders can determine if this type of strategy is right for them based on the shape of their target market, not the size of their organization. Any size of organization can implement an account-based strategy effectively if they are laser-focused on the right type of accounts that will provide a significant ROI by doing so.

————

Craig Rosenberg, Co-Founder and Chief Analyst at TOPO, Inc. shares his thoughts:

"Account based strategy works. And it works extremely well against the most important metrics to the business such as win rate, lifetime value, and deal size. There are many reasons for the success of account-based strategy:

1. Account based focuses the GTM (go-to-market) strategy on a company's most valuable accounts.

2. Alignment finally became a reality. In the TOPO Account Based Benchmark research study of account-based organizations, 90 percent said account-based improves alignment more than traditional methods.

3. Multi-touch, multi-channel orchestrated programs. Marketing, sales development, sales, executives, etc., executing coordinated touches.

So, to sum it up: an aligned organization, coordinating touches against the most valuable prospects. This is the new recipe for success."

————

6 — CONSOLIDATE SALES AND MARKETING TECH STACKS INTO A REVENUE TECH STACK

As sales and marketing tech options grow exponentially, leaders must invest in technology that enables both teams to access the same information for every target buyer and account. The Three Pillars of Alignment Transformation framework clearly states that technology's true value to the organization is the data it generates. Many of the platforms companies currently use may produce overlapping or unnecessary information. If the tech stack is viewed as a cohesive revenue tech stack, leaders can start to make tech purchasing decisions that benefit the entire Revenue Engine and provide the necessary data to make better decisions about how to engage with target buyers. Removing clutter from the tech stack helps sales and marketing teams streamline and/or eliminate unnecessary tasks from their workflows.

———

Nancy Nardin, sales technology stack expert and Co-Founder of Vendor Neutral shares her thoughts:

"With close to 8,000 marketing technologies available to choose from (yes, 8,000!), it's not easy to create an orderly and effective stack of technologies to support marketing objectives. In recent years, we've witnessed a parallel effort on the sales side. That's a good thing. There is much to be done to improve the efficiency, effectiveness, and velocity of sales. For the most part, marketing and sales technology initiatives have been done in silos. Marketing figures out their side while Sales tries to figure out theirs. You might expect that to be the approach, given that each organization has its own responsibilities and initiatives. There is a growing recognition, however, that marketing and sales do not serve two masters, but rather one. The reason marketing and sales both exist is to drive revenue. In the near term, both organizations will largely need to continue separate approaches with one important difference. They each should be asking how their technology decisions and processes impact and tie into the other. To optimize revenue, marketing and sales must ensure that technology supports alignment of the entire mission."

———

Dan Cilley, Co-Founder of Vendor Neutral shares his thoughts:

"The idea of aligning sales and marketing through technology is not a new concept; it is probably the number one driver surrounding the significant development of the B2B technology landscape. To consider not aligning these primary business development functions would be ludicrous.

There are several emerging technologies that support sales and marketing today and will well into the future. Artificial Intelligence (AI) offers the greatest potential with its ability to engage hundreds if not thousands of prospects with personalized content while simultaneously understanding how they interact with and consume it. Any effort to scale to meet this level of engagement utilizing traditional resources is not realistic or cost-effective. The sales and marketing platforms utilizing AI are evolving rapidly to match and align new insights from buyers that have not been leveraged by sales or marketing in the past.

Some of these insights could include digitized touchpoints that create meaningful value and develop trust with potential prospects and existing customers who interact with our content. With the use of Artificial Intelligence and blockchain technology, we can truly understand the customers' journey enabling new types of relationships with our prospects and customers. This new buyer-seller relationship will be one with a strong foundation of security, fairness, and equality.

Through sales innovation, we are always trying to identify new ways to communicate with each other. These future improvements in the technologies supporting sales and marketing will enable us to utilize customer insights in innovative new ways that make our existing communication between these roles even better."

---

7 — DEVELOP A CROSS-FUNCTIONAL ENABLEMENT COUNCIL

As sales and marketing become more aligned and work together with greater ease, leaders should invite other departments that contribute to the company's ability to satisfy customers' needs (i.e. product, customer success, operations, etc.) into the conversation. The creation of a cross-functional enablement council will ensure the benefits of alignment transformation are shared throughout the rest of the organization.

Roderick Jefferson, CEO of Roderick Jefferson & Associates, LLC shares share his thoughts:

"The value of developing a cross-functional enablement council lies in three areas: Communication, Collaboration, and Orchestration:

Communication

The enablement team should operate as the hub that spokes out to all other lines of business. Various types of communications are being shared by all of these LOBs (lines of business), so it requires a group to align, update, and sometimes translate the various requests and needs into "sales speak" to ensure maximum adoption and execution of tasks, activities, and deliverables.

Collaboration

The old adage of "it takes a village" has never been more true than in today's business environment. With the number of tasks, goals, and deliverables that are being executed simultaneously, enablement has the responsibility of ensuring that all parts are informed, remain on task, and are working as a cohesive unit to meet all goals, deliverables, and supporting KPIs (key performance indicators)s and metrics.

Orchestration

Notes being played at the same time sound like noise until a single conductor gets all of the musicians on the same page. It's enablement's job to act as that conductor! It has the responsibility of ensuring that all processes, programs, content, and tools are being utilized at the right time, in the right way, by the right individual to drive increased speed to revenue and continue increases in sales productivity!"

----

8 — Leverage AI to Increase Efficiency and Effectiveness

There are costs associated with generating additional revenue (e.g. increasing sales head count, adding sophisticated marketing tools and new products, etc.), so leaders need to factor these expenses into the price of competing in this new B2B economy. Presumably, increased revenue should outweigh the costs of generating new business.

Because AI (artificial intelligence) has the power to help organizations perform at a higher level of efficiency and effectiveness, companies can use it to unlock hidden insights within the CRM, help sales reps know which accounts offer the greatest potential, enable dynamic lead scoring, eliminate unnecessary tasks, create greater insights into the motivations and emotional state of target buyers, and much more. To stay competitive, leaders must learn how AI can be best leveraged in their organization.

————

Stefan Groschupf, Founder & CEO at Automation Hero shares his thoughts:

"There is absolutely no room for businesses to ignore how critical AI and automated technology is right now. But the broader aim shouldn't just be to increase revenue and cut OpEx costs but to create value for customers and meaningful work for people.

AI should augment your information workers so they can focus on value-add activities rather than wasting their time on boring, repetitive tasks.

Our goal is to make sales human again by maximizing the value that both humans and machines bring to the table. This will be the difference between companies that succeed and those that fail."

————

9 — IMPLEMENT LEAD-TO-REVENUE TRACKING (L2R)

Lead-to-Revenue Tracking (L2R) is a powerful tool that can help leadership determine which marketing activities help drive sales and contribute the most to revenue growth. L2R also enables leaders to more accurately prioritize marketing efforts based on the associated revenue generation.

L2R may seem complex when comparing the many marketing attribution models. As many as 11 different marketing attribution models exist, such as first touch, last touch, linear, time decay, u-shaped, and more. To reduce the complexity, companies new to L2R should ask the following questions that will lead them in the right direction. The answers to these types of questions will offer deeper insight into which attribution model is the best fit and put the team well on their way to leveraging L2R.

- Is our sales cycle simple or complex?

- How long is our average sales cycle?

- Do we have established and well-defined revenue funnel stages?

- Are the majority of our marketing activities conducted online or offline?

- How many marketing channels are we using to drive leads?

- What are our attribution goals?

create togetherness.™

Acknowledgments

Who knew that being frustrated with sales and marketing not understanding the potential they offer each other in achieving success would ignite my passion that led me to writing my first book. When I started focusing on the topic several years ago, I didn't have all the answers, but I knew deep down that there had to be a way to create a more productive relationship between the two. What I realized was that if we wanted to transform the dysfunctional relationship between sales and marketing into a mutually beneficial one, alignment was the answer. My mission was to develop a platform where leaders could have meaningful conversations to open themselves up to a shift in their mindsets. This shift would enable them to develop forward-thinking organizations that understand how to service the modern buyer and create togetherness.

Writing this book has been wonderful, eye-opening, and grueling simultaneously. But more than anything, I am extremely grateful that so many executives, leaders, colleagues, mentors, family, and friends have come together to support me and my work. This has been an authentic demonstration of people coming together for the greater good.

I offer a special thank you to individuals who have had a significant influence on my growth as a sales professional: Glover Johnson, Rob Hazen, Dan Harter, Craig Wortmann, Lisa Schumacher, Roderick Jefferson, Shawn Dingle, Tiffanee Smith, Hannah Fernandez, and Amir Khalil.

I also want to thank some exceptional marketers who have and will continue to inspire my passion for the art and science of marketing. Working with you has pushed me to be a better storyteller and more insightful marketer: Todd Marcero, Vikram Vaishya, Kristin Hamann, JaJa Au, Jeana Clark, Tracy Eiler, and Aurélien Gohier.

Throughout my life, I've been blessed with people who have championed me, leading to the trajectory of my career and now company. I want to express my heartfelt gratitude to each of them for pushing me to be my best self: Cindy Geisler, Eric Powell, Raymond Aronoff, Anita Brick, Shep Hyken, Keith Coleman, Mark Ferguson, Andy Strandmark, Jeff Rosset, Mary Shea, Waverly Deutsch, Matt Ostanik, Jon Borg-Breen, Ed Ross, Chris Robinson, Jonathan Delgado, Jonathan Salinas, Gene Finley, and Brigitte Anderson.

And, a huge thank you to those who offered an immense amount of support in both the creation of this book and in life: Alfredo Marulanda, Jarred Davis, the original Jeff Davis (my dad), Sean Lenard, Dionne (Hudson) Gardner, Shaelyn Otikor, Loretta Kelly, Todd Caponi, and Ryan Leavitt.

Each one of you has been a champion for me in many different ways. Your generosity and support have created a path that I don't think I would have ever been able to manifest on my own. I will forever be grateful for how you've enriched my life.

I also want to thank each guest I've had the pleasure of interviewing on *TheAlignmentPodcast.com*. Your willingness to contribute your invaluable wisdom and expertise to this platform motivates and inspires me to do even more for this community of B2B leaders.

And, a huge shout out to my audio engineer - Chris "KID" Robinson. I literally couldn't produce the show without him.

THE ALIGNMENTPODCAST.COM ROSTER

Tracy Eiler: Ep. 02 - Marketing Exists to Make Sales Easier

Anthony Iannarino: Ep. 03 - Higher-Value Conversations Lead To More Deals

Debra Mashek, Ph.D: Ep. 04 - The Psychology of Collaboration

Ted Corbeill: Ep. 05 – Be Insight-Driven, Not Just Data-Driven

Trish Bertuzzi: Ep. 06 – Hey, CEO! You Are Responsible For Alignment

Dan Cilley: Ep. 07 – How To Develop The Best Revenue Tech Stack

Justin Shriber: Ep. 08 – Customer Experience Is The Future of B2B

David Coleman: Ep. 09 – Digital Transformation Is Forcing Alignment

Roderick Jefferson: Ep. 10 – Decreasing Time To Revenue Requires A Focus On Customer Value

Peter Strohkorb: Ep. 11 – Fix Misalignment By Identifying The Root Cause

Mike Schultz: Ep. 12 – Buyers Want To Hear From You Early In Their Journey

Nancy Nardin: Ep. 13 – How To Choose The Right Sales Tech

Moran Cerf, Ph.D.: Ep. 14 – Using Neuroscience to Understand Human Collaboration

Maggie Sarfo: Ep. 15 – Get More Buy-in By Connecting Alignment With Business Strategy

Todd Caponi: Ep. 16 – Leverage Transparency To Shorten Sales Cycles

Peter Isaacson: Ep. 33 – Should We Kill The Marketing Qualified Lead?

Gabe Larsen: Ep. 34 – How AI Increases Competitiveness

Joel Harrison: Ep. 35 – The Future Of B2B Marketing

Ron Carucci: Ep. 36 – Changing The Dysfunctional Sales and Marketing Narrative

Rob Kall: Ep. 37 – Quantifying Misalignment's Impact On Growth

Craig Rosenberg: Ep. 38 – 5 Elements Of A Bulletproof Account-Based Strategy

Dave Elkington: Ep. 39 - How To Make Better Decisions Using The Right B2B Data

About the Author

Jeff Davis, international speaker and founder of JD2 Consulting Group, specializes in helping B2B companies strategically align their sales and marketing teams to accelerate revenue growth. Jeff pulls from his more than 15 years of experience in sales, marketing, and business development at *Fortune* 100 organizations to early-stage startups. He has experience in a myriad of different industries including healthcare, biotech, manufacturing, industrial products, technology, aerospace and more. Jeff has worked with companies such as Salesforce, LinkedIn, Seismic, InsideSales.com, and Oracle. He speaks regularly on the topic of alignment transformation at large conferences, company meetings, sales kick-offs, association meetings, and more. He is also the executive producer and host of the fast-growing *TheAlignmentPodcast.com* which is heard by B2B professionals in over 25 countries, as well as the creator and host of the Sales + Marketing Alignment Summit™ which has hosted an exclusive group of sales and marketing leaders for the past four years. Jeff holds a B.S. in Mechanical Engineering from Purdue University and an MBA from The University of Chicago Booth School of Business. He is available for keynote speaking, consulting engagements, and media appearances.

You can connect with Jeff at:

🌐 meetjeffdavis.com

✉ jeff@jeffdavis2.com

in /in/jeffreydavisii

🐦 @jeff_davis2

📷 @alignwithjeffdavis

Index

I

J

K

L

M

Made in USA - Kendallville, IN
93245_9781733450409
09.03.2022 1244